# THE
# COMPLETE
# GUNDOG TRAINING
# MANUAL

# THE
# COMPLETE
# GUNDOG TRAINING
# MANUAL

## James Douglas

SWAN·HILL
PRESS

# DEDICATION

This book is dedicated to everyone who enjoys working with gundogs, and to my family and friends who put up with my faults and excesses.

It is also dedicated to those who enjoy the wild places, who value all wildlife. We must look after it – it is precious and our children depend on us to protect and keep it for them.

First published in the UK in 2003
by Swan Hill Press, an imprint of Quiller Publishing Ltd

**British Library Cataloguing-in-Publication Data**
A catalogue record for this book
is available form the British Library

ISBN 0 904057 05 5

Printed in England by The Bath Press Ltd., Bath.

## Swan Hill Press

an imprint of Quiller Publishing Ltd.
Wykey House, Wykey, Shrewsbury, SY4 1JA, England
Tel: 01939 261616  Fax: 01939 261606
E-mail: info@quillerbooks.com
Website: www.swanhillbooks.com

# CONTENTS

# ACKNOWLEDGEMENTS

I wish to thank Donald Sherwood who not only posed for some of the photographs with his dogs but gave me invaluable help with the chapter on older dogs.

# 1
# INTRODUCTION

Whether you shoot driven birds in the south of England or hunt wild pheasants in Kansas, whether you are a wildfowler on the Wash or Solway, or a duck and goose hunter in Chesapeake or the southern wetlands, the one thing that we all share is the need for a good dog.

Your dog adds so much in both pleasure and companionship to your time outdoors. He is a necessary part of what makes your time in the field fruitful, rewarding and enjoyable. A good dog can make a huge contribution to your pleasure in the outdoors, a bad dog is a liability, and can ruin your day.

*James Douglas stalking rabbits with a well behaved Labrador.* (LYLE MITCHELL)

*Gundogs and owners at a James Douglas training clinic.* (JAMES DOUGLAS)

I believe that anyone with a little determination and proper guidance can train their dog to a high standard. If you have a young dog and are prepared to put in the effort, you will derive a great deal of pleasure from training and educating him; creating the sort of working companion that will pay you back a thousand fold by giving you years of pleasure. With a little effort (and a good book) you can produce a canine companion who is a dog of whom you can really be proud.

One of the problems that most people encounter when they first start training their dog is getting good advice. Often well-meaning friends and so-called 'experts' do more harm than good with their advice. So where do you turn for guidance? There are many books on the market – some are excellent and others are not. Most make the assumption that you already know what you're doing and have access to the same facilities as the author. They may have been written by experts in dog training but often the authors do not have the ability to communicate in a manner which is easily understood, the implication being that the subject is so complicated that you require special skills to master it. All this results in is to discourage and dishearten the new dog owner.

Then of course there are videos. I am fortunate in that my videos on gundog training and field sports have been consistent best sellers. Although video has the advantage in that it can show the viewer how to approach a particular subject in a visual and easily understood manner they have the drawback of being time-limited. To cover the multitude of subjects in a video that I can in this book, would make a ridiculously long series of videos.

I have been training dogs for many years, and have trained every one of the gundog breeds. I have worked with and trained virtually every breed of dog. Over the years I have experienced just about every problem a dog can have and how it to deal with it.

Whilst I believe that anyone with the will and a little guidance can train a dog, I also believe that some of us are lucky enough to have more empathy with these animals. As a child my parents always had family dogs and from my earliest recollections I can remember being interested in trying to teach them tricks. Adults would say that I had some special understanding with dogs. Some of us seem to have a special connection which helps dogs to relate to us better than others.

I have seen this phenomenon several times. Possibly the best example is with one of my own sons. Even when he was small our dogs seemed to be naturally drawn towards him. Indeed my own favourite gundog bitch would be completely oblivious to me the minute he appeared. She would follow him around as though I didn't exist.

For many years I have studied canine behavioural patterns and canine body language. Like humans dogs are all individuals with their own likes and dislikes and the little idiosyncrasies that make each dog a challenge to communicate with, to help it to use its brain, and to achieve its full potential.

# 2
# UNDERSTANDING THE MIND OF YOUR DOG

**'You can take the dog out of the pack but not the pack out of the dog'**

To understand fully the mind of your dog and why your dog wants to work for you, to get the best out of your dog, whether the dog is a family pet or is intended to be a high performance working dog, it is important that you have an understanding of what motivates your dog, how it thinks and what its natural instincts and needs are.

Irrespective of the breed of dog, whether it is a Labrador Retriever, a Springer Spaniel, a German Shepherd, or a Border Collie, whether the task required of the dog is retrieving a bird, flushing a rabbit, finding a criminal in a darkened factory at night, or rounding up a flock of sheep, the dogs all share one common aspect of their behaviour – they want to work for the handler!

But what is it that allows this group of animals to so relate to humans that we can teach them to work for us? Horses also work for us, but they are harnessed into the traces, we have them pull a carriage or we put a saddle on their backs and a bit in their mouths and ride them. We have domesticated them and make use of their abilities. But no matter how much we like them, or that they show recognition and indeed pleasure with our association, they are fundamentally beasts of burden.

Dogs on the other hand work for us in such a wide variety of tasks because they want to. We are using their instincts and they get pleasure from working with us as gundogs or bomb dogs, drug dogs, sheepdogs, mountain rescue dogs, carriage dogs, or guard dogs. Over the centuries breeds have been developed to perform many diverse tasks.

Since early history we have had an association with dogs. Why? As far as we humans are concerned the answer is easy – dogs give us unquestioning loyalty and companionship, and most important of all – and the reason we have developed this relationship with the canine world – they do our bidding! They work for us without complaint, asking little in return.

But why do dogs work for us? Dogs in their natural state would live in packs like their closest relatives, wolves. To understand fully why dogs work for us you have to look at the structure of the wolf pack. A young animal growing up in a pack enjoys the security of living in association with others older and wiser than him. It is through them that he learns the ways of the world. It is with the help and assistance of other members of the pack that he can hunt and eat as he grows toward becoming an adult member of the pack. A canine is a pack animal, he is a social animal enjoying that company of others off his kind. A dog – just like a wolf – functions best as part of a group.

*This Cocker Spaniel is alert and ready to do its owner's bidding.* (DAVID HUDSON)

To watch a wolf pack hunt it is obvious they have some communicative ability. They work together with co-operation, the individuals working not only for their own good but for the collective good of the pack. While a wolf pack might roam over a vast area, they are territorial, and they will mark their territory by scenting it with urine and faeces. They will defend their territory with ferocity. When you look at the natural instincts of a wolf you begin to see the basis of how a domestic dog behaves.

The wolf pack evolved to live as a harmonious group, where there would be a pecking order – a hierarchy of senior pack members – denoted primarily by age, a structure of discipline within the pack and an ultimate authority, the pack leader, or the Alpha male. If we wish to understand why a dog works for us, we need to look at the natural instincts of the canine. The tasks we use them for are only extensions of the natural instincts that they would display within the structure of the pack. It is quite simple, all the tasks that we train dogs to do are merely variations of their hunting instincts.

It is important that we understand the key words 'discipline' and 'co-operation' in a wolf pack , or in a pack of wild dogs. Whilst there is always bickering – particularly at feeding time – there are seldom serious fights or damage caused to each other by pack members. The pecking order works. The pack leaders eat first, snarling and threatening those younger members that try to take the food out of turn. Only when the pack leaders, the Alpha male and Alpha female, have taken several mouthfuls will some of the lower ranking members of the pack approach, with bodies lowered, heads down and ears back, asking to be allowed to feed.

If you spend time watching a wolf pack, you will sometimes see a young male stepping out of line and an argument ensues between the young wolf and an older male. Much snarling and baring of teeth is normally enough to put the young wolf in its place. If it doesn't comply the older male will instantly set about the younger wolf, but it is rare for real damage to be done as a few nips are normally enough to enforce discipline.

To understand fully your dog's behaviour and body language, and the sounds that he makes one need only look at the behaviour of the wolf pack. A wolf's first loyalty is always to the pack which may number anything from eight to thirty, the numbers that make-up the pack governed by the food sources available. It is nature's way of practising birth control – wherever a prey species is numerous, predator numbers increase. Equally, when the food source is scarce numbers reduce, the number of offspring born reduces, and the weaker members of any predatory group die off. It is simply the survival of the fittest.

The pack is always led by a dominant male, the Alpha male. He is very much the leader of the pack and all other males defer to him. Equally, there is an Alpha female to whom all the females submit. Next in rank in the pack are the Beta male and Beta female. Every wolf in the pack has their place and must submit to any wolf of higher rank. This structure of discipline is like a ladder system with each member of the pack occupying his or her place down to the bottom of the pecking order which is occupied by the Omega male and Omega female.

The concept of 'equal' does not exist in the canine world, whether dog or wolf, it is either dominant or submissive. Wolves are continuously demonstrating their rank over the others in the pack and have an extensive body language – a whole series of movements which announce their mood to the others of the pack. It is by observing and learning their body language that you can quickly read their mood. On meeting a member of the pack a higher ranking wolf would normally show his superiority and confidence by raising his tail, putting his ears forward, and aggressively snarling, raising his hackles to make himself look as a big and threatening as possible. The lower ranking wolf will show his subservience by making himself look as non-threatening and small as he can, dropping his ears flat back, his tail tucked under his belly. He will try licking the higher ranking wolf's muzzle; he will grovel, flattening himself onto the ground or roll onto his back. This acknowledgement of a higher ranking wolf's position is normally enough to avoid a fight. Wolves try to avoid actually fighting with each other since any serious injury would impair their ability to hunt.

Wolves have a system of communication to signal their status, mood or intentions to each other through body language. A tail held erect with all four legs straightened with head held high as the wolf stands as tall as he can, shows dominance. Body lowered, tail between legs or held low and pawing at the other wolf is an acknowledgement of the other's superiority. Ears flattened against the head shows fear. Ears lifted straight up, lips curled back showing teeth displays anger. Rolling on the back is submission.

A body language of shoulder bumps, bodies standing side by side, arched backs, lowered backs, hip curved towards head, walking sideways, tail flopping, tail erect, tail wagging, tongue flicking, staring eyes, slant eyes, eyes downcast, all communicate their different moods. The intention to play can be seen by dancing around, dropping their front end into a crouch position, tail wagging and an almost smiling face.

Just like their dog cousins wolves can also communicate through scent and sound. They will dribble small amounts of urine at various points around their territory, a signal to show any others outside of their own group that this is their property. Then of course they have their voice – barking, yipping, squeaks, whimpers, howling, and a variety of grunts and squeaks – even these sounds can be broken into a variety of different tones. A bark can be full-throated and intimidating, it can be short and higher pitched to draw attention or it can signal danger. Wolves will howl for a variety of reasons but the obvious and principal reason is to communicate with other pack members. Dogs howl (normally when they are lonely) if they feel abandoned and are on their own. This is where their wolf instincts come to the surface. They will throw their heads back and howl in an attempt to announce their presence and hopefully this will bring them company.

A wolf pack it is an example of a cohesive group of animals working with communication and association with each other within a structure of discipline, for their collective and individual benefit and survival. For the pack to work there must be that key word 'discipline'.

You will no doubt by now have recognized many of the behavioural similarities I have described with wolves and your own dog. The more you observe your dog the more you will learn

*The yellow Labrador is the dominant dog here even though it is younger than the chocolate Labrador.*
(DAVID HUDSON)

*Gordon Setter with handler at a field trial: partners, but the handler must always play the role of Alpha male, or pack leader.* (DAVID HUDSON)

to read its body language. If you bring a young dog into your home to live with you and your family you place it into an environment which – no matter how domesticated the animal is – is foreign to the dog's nature. You have to teach the dog what is acceptable behaviour. You must teach it, for instance, not to defecate on the floor. Initially you are taking the place of its mother, then as the puppy grows into a young dog you take the place of the pack leader.

If you try to humanize your young dog, attributing emotions to it that it cannot possibly understand, if you try to make it a member of your family, disaster will almost certainly follow. You will give the dog confusing and conflicting signals, foreign to the natural way that its mind works. The dog will never achieve its full potential as a working dog. I am not suggesting that the dog cannot live with and give much pleasure to you and your family, but you must remember that it is a pack animal and must be shown its place in the pack. The secret of training any dog is consistency and 'discipline'. The handler must become the Alpha male and use the young dog's desire to co-operate with the pack leader.

As a professional trainer I have, in the course of my working year, many problem dogs brought to me – not just gun dogs – but a wide variety of different breeds that are domestic pets who are giving their owners' problems. These problems range from simple pulling on the lead to aggression. Irrespective of the breed or problems that the individual dogs have, 99 per cent are simply suffering from a lack of discipline and have received confusing signals. After I have had their dog for a few minutes the owners often remark that the dog seems to respond to me quicker and better than it does for them. Indeed that their dog is actually more comfortable with me than it is with them.

There is a simple explanation for this canine behaviour. Because of my familiarity with dogs and the fact that I am comfortable with them, I do not represent a threat, yet the dog instinctively recognizes me as the Alpha male. He feels comfortable and safe in the presence of the pack leader. Everyone has heard the old wives' tale that a dog knows if you're afraid of it. It's true. If you are afraid you exude pheromones, giving off a signal that the dog will quickly pick up. Equally, however, if you wish the dog no harm but are very much the confident pack leader, the dog instinctively knows this. There are occasions of course when a dog might wish to challenge me, but this is easily overcome by simply knowing how to react.

I have experienced this on many hundreds of occasions. However one example stands out. I was filming a television programme on the origins of the Chesapeake Bay Retriever on location near the Blackwater reserve in Maryland on the east coast of the United States. We needed access to a good quality representative of the breed so after a few phone calls to arrange things I arrived with the camera crew at a shooting reserve where the manager had a big working Chesapeake male.

Bubba was fours year old, bad mannered and half trained. His owner looked at me and grinned, telling me that Bubba would never work for or respond to me. We needed to get on with the filming so I dropped my rope lead round the dog's neck and walked away across a field, giving him a few discreet hard jerks on the rope. I did not want either the owner or the camera crew to hear what I was saying. I spoke to the dog for a few moments then set off back towards the crew. The dog was so keen to walk at my heel he was pushing his shoulder against my leg, almost knocking me over.

By the time I walked back the crew were set up and ready to start filming. I stood Bubba side-on to the camera and started talking about the breed's conformation and development. By now the owner, no longer able to contain himself, blurted out 'I don't know what you've done to my dog he never stood like that before'. What I had said it to the dog is not important, it was the manner in which I had spoken and the way I had behaved that was the key. The dog had simply accepted the fact that I was the Alpha male and he was my new pal!

Another excellent example of a dog picking up on pheromones or what might be described as 'canine body language' is an experience I once had in Zimbabwe in Africa. I had just arrived with a group of friends at a hunting camp in the bush and as we were unpacking our luggage from the vehicle that had brought us from the airport, I turned round just in time to see a big dark yellow dog start to lift his leg on one of the suitcases. Without stopping to think I snarled at the dog and cracked him across the hindquarters. He turned and gave me a baleful look with his cold little eyes, I recognized immediately that this was one dog that was unused to being spoken to or hit as I had just done. We both stood sizing each other up as I thought what a handsome creature he looked. I wasn't sure whether he was a mixture of Labrador and Mastiff or what he was. I discovered later he was a Boer Bull by the name of Danni.

Danni followed me to the little cabin I was staying in and, while I unpacked, he waited outside the door. Then he followed me across the lawn when I went to join my friends and have a welcome drink. His owner, who paid him very little attention and not once whilst I was there showed him any affection, told me that he was the camp guard dog. The big dog followed me round for the rest of the day, and when I was on my own I talked to him and stroked his ears. At dinner that night he lay beside my chair and I gave him a few table scraps.

For the three weeks of my stay at the camp I had a constant shadow. The big Boer Bull would lie across the doorway of my cabin at night and growl menacingly if anyone came near. During the day he followed me everywhere. If I left the camp in a vehicle he simply waited patiently until I returned, then attached himself to me once again. This was a perfect example of a dog recognizing the Alpha male and at the same time getting the attention that he needed.

## How it all began

Dogs have been with us as part of our lives for so long that to understand how it all began you really must make an educated guess. From what we know from the earliest recorded history – whether it be the Greeks, the Romans, the Egyptians, or the ancient British – they all had dogs as part of their lives which they used primarily for hunting.

The Saluki was domesticated as early has 329BC. In Britain between AD61 and AD63 Queen Boadicea of the Iceni Celts, who led her troops against the invading Romans, had, as part of her defence, couples of Mastiffs.

But how did it all begin? Imagine some early settlement of humans sitting eating meat. In the background, attracted by the smell, some wild dogs hang about, scavenging any bones discarded by the humans. It would not take long before the dogs realized that by staying close to the humans they might get some scraps. The dogs, with their superior hearing, would hear the approach of wild beasts and snarl or bark to protect their territory, and the humans would see advantage in having the dogs around.

The dogs would follow the humans as they moved about. They would soon learn that if they followed the humans when they went hunting they would get more scraps. If a man got a spear or an arrow into an animal, the dogs would quickly learn to follow the blood, and with their ability to run much faster than the men they would catch the animal before the men. When they arrived

the men would beat off the dogs and take the carcass.

It would be long before both man and dog would see the advantage in this association and gradually they would learn to depend upon each other for mutual advantage. The rest is history.

But wait, you might think, would the dogs not have hunted the men? That is highly unlikely. Possibly the smell of man frightened the dogs but why they would not attack them is difficult to theorize. What is true, however, is that despite all the horror stories surrounding the dog's nearest relative – the wolf – there has never been any recorded incidence of a wolf attacking a human being throughout North America. We're not regarded as a prey species. Whatever the reason, the relationship between man and dog is one of mutual benefit. It suits us both and we both gain from the association.

As men began to realize that dogs had specific talents and behavioural patterns, the idea of selectively breeding to enforce and pronounce the desired abilities of the dogs eventually caught on and over

*Golden Retriever and handler learning to work as a team at a James Douglas training clinic.* (JAMES DOUGLAS)

centuries dogs have been bred to combine their most desirable tendencies.

## Why so many breeds?

You might ask yourself why there is such a variety of different sizes and types of dog with such a diverse range of body shapes. The answer is simple. Over many hundreds (or even thousands) of years men have selectively bred them to develop specific attributes, tendencies and abilities, some of which are very unusual.

The Dogue de Bordeaux has its origins in one the most ancient breeds, with a more recently descent from the Alaunt, a breed introduced to France during the Middle Ages from the Orient. The Dogue de Bordeaux is huge and was used to fight both gladiators and wild beasts in the amphitheatres of ancient Rome. The Mastiff that we know today in Britain and the US descends from this bloodline.

The Lundehund originated above the Arctic Circle in the Lofoten Archipelago, specifically the island of Vaeroy, and is possibly the world's most unusual and rarest dog. It is believed to have survived the last glacial era in Norway with puffins becoming its principal source of food. A particular oddity about this breed is that it has fewer teeth than most dogs and two extra toes. This little dog was traditionally used by islanders to harvest both puffin eggs and well-grown chicks which were preserved and used as a food source.

We now have a rich variety of breeds of gun dog, each with particular talents and abilities to suit the individual sporting environment.

# 3

# WHAT IS THE BEST BREED FOR ME?

The early shotguns were muzzleloaders, used by wealthy landowners who controlled much of the land and sport – particularly the vast moorland areas. Since the muzzleloader was essentially a weapon which took some time to load between shots, and since the majority of shooting was practised on vast open areas, the ideal dogs for the early shotgunner were the pointers and setters. These dogs had been developed for their physical abilities to cover large areas of land, ranging in front of the gun until they scented game. Then they took a set or point, indicating the presence of game and giving the shooter ample time to make his way to the dog, and when he was ready, flush the game.

*Early muzzle-loading shotguns were slow to load and produced dense clouds of smoke when fired.*
(DAVID HUDSON)

It was the invention of the breechloader – a much faster method of shooting – that marked the decline in popularity and use of pointers and setters. For the breechloader made it possible for driven shooting to develop, and now a dog that would spring game from cover was required, one that would 'busy about' flushing game, sending it out and away towards the standing guns. The breechloader also made it less important for the shooter to have warning of the game's impending presence. It was now possible for a dog to 'busy down' a hedgerow flushing game in front of his handler. And the spaniels came into their own.

As greater numbers of game were shot this opened the door for the specialist retrievers who were the stylish experts at finding and picking lost and wounded game. As the sport of shooting increased in popularity across the social spectrum, so the types of shooting continued to diversify, with more and more sportsmen enjoying the particular type of shooting that took their fancy – grouse, ground game, or wildfowling. Add to this the personal preferences that individuals had for one breed or another and the future was assured for many breeds of dog.

Whilst British sporting dog enthusiasts continued to strive to produce the highest possible standards in the various different breeds that they themselves most preferred, they never tried to combine the attributes, rather concentrating on keeping their breeds pure and singular in purpose. It was the continental shooters who developed the breeds that were intended to perform all the functions that the three types of British gundog – hunters, pointers and retrievers – did so well, and so the HPR (hunting, pointing, retrieving) breeds were established.

The idea of a dog that could do all three jobs was a good one. The basic reason that the continental sportsmen saw the need for such a dog was that they were likely to encounter a greater range of game in a day than his counterpart was in Britain – boar, deer or game birds. And just as they developed a gun known as a drilling, which was a combination of rifle and shotgun barrels clustered together to accommodate all game, so also did they develop multi-purpose dogs. These were dogs with the versatility to range in front of the hunter, to point and hold game, then to retrieve the game from either land or water.

If the game was large or wounded, the dog was able to track it through the dense European forests. The dog was able to keep up a good fast pace all day, in any terrain and to be everything that the *jäger* could possibly wish for in a dog.

The continentals also had a different attitude towards field sports. In Britain we developed a tradition of *either* going stalking for deer with a rifle, or shooting birds with a shotgun. Anyone who has witnessed some of the traditions and ceremonies that surround much of the sporting activities on the continent would see that great emphasis is placed on the seriousness of the activity and a greater appreciation for the ultimate plight of quarry than we display in Britain. To be fair however, much of Germany and Hungary is covered with large forests, and a wounded animal could speedily vanish into the dense cover, so a dog that was adept at following a trail obviously had its uses. And if the same dog also had the ability to retrieve a bird from water, then there was no need to own two animals.

There are many claims made by dog enthusiasts about the abilities of their favoured breed of gundog. Most dog owners tend to think that their particular favourite is supreme. The sensible potential dog owner, however, should think carefully about the type of shooting he does, and which dog would best suit his needs. Combine this with the breed that he finds attractive and that is the one to choose. I firmly believe that a large part of owning and successfully training a gundog is that you like his looks.

## Spaniels

### English Springer Spaniel

To see a good English Springer Spaniel (ESS) as he works away merrily, quartering in front of the gun, dropping to flush as he 'springs' game, dashing forward on command to retrieve shot game, and bringing it back to the handler, is a joy to anyone who is interested in gundogs of any kind, for the Springer is indeed a most useful and exciting little dog But it has been said that whilst you can put up with a half-trained Labrador and learn to live with it, a half-trained Springer can be an uncontrolled nightmare. This can be true of any dog, but the reason it is said with regard to Springers is that by the very nature of his character and type of work, he is a busy little dog, whizzing through cover. If he is not trained to harness his energy into a controlled work pattern, he can quickly get out of control and end up running wild.

The Springer is probably the oldest of the 'land' spaniels. One theory is that they may have been first brought to Britain by the Romans. Remembering that the Romans are credited with the introduction of the fallow deer, which were brought to Britain as a food source, it is entirely possible that they would have brought their dogs with them. The name 'spaniel', however, refers to the generally accepted theory that they originated in Spain. It is certain that they were in Britain five hundred years ago, since a Dr Cauis, personal physician to Edward VI, and also a dog enthusiast, wrote in his mid-sixteenth century *History of English Dogges* of the origin of the Springer, describing a dog that sprang game for the hunter. It is also certain that the Springers of today are the product of many serious breeding experiments over many years. It would be true to say that of all the types of spaniel in use as gundogs, the Springer is

*A classic young working English Springer Spaniel.* (JAMES DOUGLAS)

certainly the most versatile and widely used, and the general image of many rough shooters and countrymen is one of them with a Springer at heel.

The Springer is certainly the best of the hunting dogs in Britain, yet has the ability to retrieve from both land and water. The Springer has very much developed into two distinct strains of dog – working and show – and whilst with other breeds such as the Curly-coated and Flat-coated Retrievers it can be difficult for the potential buyer to find a strain of dog that is entirely work bred (many of them being dual dogs used for both show-bench and work), with the Springer this is not the case. The working Springer differs considerably from the breed standard, and in show Springers much of the working instinct has been lost. So it is imperative that anyone who wishes to buy a Springer Spaniel for the gun must satisfy himself that the dog is from an impeccable working pedigree.

## Welsh Springer Spaniel

To non-Springer Spaniel enthusiasts the Welsh and English Springers are normally lumped together simply as Springers, yet they are in fact two entirely different breeds, with certain differences between them. The Welsh Springer is more difficult to train in that he is more intent on hunting away, and a great deal of care and patience must be taken to keep his attention. Smaller than the English Springer, his coat is of a dark rich red and white colouration. The Welsh Springer is a fabulously energetic little dog, and as far as work is concerned there is little to choose between either the English or the Welsh. Unfortunately however, true working strains are not as easily found in the Welsh Springers as their larger English cousins.

## Cocker Spaniel

The Cocker Spaniel is descended from the same ancestors as the Springer. Although there are references to Cockers or cocking spaniels going back several centuries it was not until the beginning of the twentieth century that Springers and Cockers were finally separated into two distinct breeds. At one time the difference between what the Kennel Club recognized as a Springer or a Cocker was solely weight: a dog weighing less than about twenty-eight pounds was a Cocker: anything over that weight was a Springer.

Now though the little Cocker can be distinguished from its larger cousin by its size, its looks and its character. Busy, bustling and eager, Cockers hunt with tremendous enthusiasm and will tackle the thickest of cover with apparent indifference to thorn or bramble. Most have a mischievous side to their nature that can make training and handling them something of an adventure, but their sheer delight in working for the gun or in the beating line makes up for the occasional little indiscretion. They will retrieve fur or feather from land or water, happily tackling a cock pheasant even though it looks almost as big as themselves.

As with the Springer, the Cocker Spaniel is sharply divided between show and working strains and it is essential that anyone wanting a Cocker Spaniel as a shooting dog ensures that it comes from working parents and not from show lines.

## Minor Breed Spaniels

In addition to the Springer, the Welsh Springer and the Cocker there are four other working spaniel breeds: the Clumber Spaniel, the Sussex Spaniel, the Field Spaniel and the Irish Water Spaniel. These are generally classified as 'minor breed' spaniels because they are much less

*Eager and alert: a Cocker Spaniel working on a grouse moor.* (DAVID HUDSON)

common than the other three breeds. Indeed, while Springers and Cockers can be seen working on shoots the length and breadth of the country, it is, to say the very least, unusual to see any of the other breeds working. That said, it is still possible to find good working examples of all four minor breeds, and Minor Breed field trials are held each year specifically for Clumbers, Sussex and Field Spaniels.

## Clumber Spaniel

The Clumber is a much bigger and heavier dog than any of the other spaniel breeds with the exception of the Irish Water Spaniel. The Clumber has a long, heavy body, a broad, strong head and short but powerful legs. Their thick coat is predominantly white with orange or lemon markings and they have a steady, rolling gait quite unlike any of the other spaniel breeds. They are named for Clumber Park in Nottinghamshire and are reputed to have originated as a gift to the Duke of Newcastle from the Duc de Noailles.

They work at a much more deliberate pace than the Springer or Cocker and generally have a quieter, less excitable nature than most spaniel breeds. With their slower pace they may take longer to find game than a thrusting Springer but on days when scent is poor it is claimed that they are less likely to miss birds than the faster workers. Their placid nature suits them well for work as retrievers on driven game shoots where they will happily sit quietly at a peg – something which tests the patience of even the best trained Cocker.

## Field Spaniel

The term 'Field Spaniel' was used by some writers in the nineteenth century as a blanket term to distinguish 'land' spaniels from 'water' spaniels. Today the Field Spaniel is a breed in its own right, though it originates from the same stock as Springers and Cockers. The breed was the victim of some disastrous experimentation at the end of the nineteenth and beginning of the twentieth centuries with blood from various other breeds being introduced to try to 'improve' various characteristics of its work or appearance. Irish Water Spaniel, Irish Setter and even Bassett Hound crosses were tried, often with predictably awful results. The breed has since recovered from these indignities and stabilized into an exceptionally handsome dog about the size and build of a Springer with a steady, calm temperament. They are usually solid coloured liver, black or tan though roan examples are also found.

It is not easy to find Field Spaniels from proven working stock but they do exist and are capable of good, solid work in the shooting field. With their good looks and steady nature it is surprising that they are not seen more often working for the gun though this is probably a reflection of the difficulty in finding a working Field Spaniel compared with the ease of locating Springers or Cockers from proven stock.

## Sussex Spaniel

The Sussex Spaniel is the least common of the minor breeds. They come somewhere between the Clumber and the Field Spaniel in appearance, being solidly built dogs with short, strong legs and a thick golden coat that makes them particularly suitable for water work. The breed was almost extinct at the end of the Second World War but has made a gradual comeback since then, mainly in the hands of show breeders.

Their reputation in the shooting field is as steady but determined workers with good stamina and the courage to face cover. They are said to be easy to train and keen to please their owners. They are alone among the spaniel breeds in being expected to give tongue while working – something that, while not unknown among the other spaniels, is considered a fault with most gundog breeds.

## Irish Water Spaniel

The Irish Water Spaniel is something of an anomaly among the spaniel classification as it is built more along the lines of the retrieving breeds such as the Flat-coat or Labrador being much longer on the leg than any other spaniel and looking somewhat like a Curly-coated Retriever. They have a thick, brown, oily coat, which grows in tight curls apart from on their faces and tails, and, as the name implies, are superb retrievers from water. They used to enjoy great popularity among wildfowlers, though now the Labrador or the Chesapeake Bay Retriever is a more likely sight on the foreshore.

At one time they were classed with the spaniels for field trial purposes and competed in spaniel trials, where the emphasis is more on game-finding than on retrieving. In 1985 the Kennel Club re-classified them as retrievers and those that compete in field trials now take part in retriever trials. They will certainly work in a beating line or for a walking gun, but it is as retrievers that they are at their best and particularly where the retrieving involves water or wet, boggy ground.

# Retrievers

## *Chesapeake Bay Retriever*

The origins of the Chesapeake Bay Retriever, also knows as the American Duck Retriever, reads like an episode from a period drama. There are several versions of how the breed originated, and although they all differ slightly, they tie together with the relevant names and places.

In the early 1880s an English brig set sail from Newfoundland. On board were two Newfoundland puppies, a dog and a bitch. Off the coast of Maryland the ship started to take water and founder, but an American ship, the *Canton* from the port of Baltimore, rescued the crew and the two puppies. The dog, which is said to have been a dirty red colour and called 'Sailor' was handed over to a Mr James Mercer of West River, and the bitch, who was said to have a black coat, was given to a Dr James Stewart of Sparrow Point. Both dogs were compact, strongly built animals, although not quite as large as Newfoundland puppies of the same age would have been expected to be. They had medium length coats with thick wavy hair.

At this point the details of the story become sketchy, but the two dogs apparently achieved some considerable local attention in the Chesapeake area as duck dogs, and it is assumed that these two dogs (though there are no records to show that they were ever bred together) were put together with local retrievers and hound stock, from which it is accepted the Chesapeake Bay Retriever evolved. Flat-coated and Curly-coated Retrievers, and the local otter hounds, all possibly added their blood to the development of the breed.

There is, however, another version of the story that I prefer and which holds more credibility and was recounted by General Ferdinand C. Latrobe, a one-time mayor of Baltimore. This story claims that the English vessel unfortunately grounded in the coastal waters lying off the Walnut Grove Estate, which is situated on the banks of the Chesapeake River. This estate was the home of a well-known and established New England family, headed by a Mr John Law. As a gesture of gratitude for his help in saving the crew – and the hospitality they were shown on the estate – the two puppies from the English vessel were presented to John Law. There the puppies remained in the estate kennel and were bred with the local hounds. The eventual introduction of many different water spaniel strains, is the most likely and credible source of many of the Chesapeake's attributes of stamina, scenting power and of course colouration – which is a yellowy liver colour.

The Chesapeake Bay Retriever is an utterly superb and highly specialized water dog. His development has suited him quite perfectly for his environment. The outer coat is highly water resistant, harsh to the touch, tight and distinctly wavy, with an undercoat of a soft dense oily consistency, which gives the coat an almost total water resistance. In company with the Labrador, the Chesapeake shares the distinction of being one of the two dogs popularly used by the American market gunners of the east coast of America. Unfortunately the Chesapeake is not common in Europe, and the chances of British field sportsmen managing to find top class working Chesapeakes are slim.

## *Labrador Retriever*

For good reason the Labrador Retriever is the most popular and widely accepted retrieving dog in Britain, for this breed is truly the master of all forms of retrieving, whether in the high grouse moor or fowling in the harsh coastal areas.

Originally referred to as the St John's Breed from Newfoundland, the breed was probably brought to Britain during the nineteenth century aboard ships trading from the North-eastern Seaboard of America, particularly from Newfoundland and the Labrador coast. These vessels landed their cargoes on the West Coast ports of Britain, including the Clyde in Scotland and Poole in Dorset. When one understands the highly privileged society of the nineteenth century, when the landed gentry spent much of their time in the pursuit of game and all things sporting, it is easy to understand how these breeds found their way into the hands of the noble families.

The second Earl of Malmesbury, who had an estate near Poole, is known to have acquired one of these dogs, which was taken to work on his sporting estate. So impressed was he by the dog's general abilities as a fieldsports dog that the family bought other specimens of the breed and set up their own small population at the estate kennel, keeping the breed as pure as possible. It was the third Earl who referred to the breed as his 'Labradors'.

The Dukes of Hamilton and Buccleuch, and the Earl of Home all had estates in the region of Scotland to the south of the River Clyde, and it is

*Yellow Labrador: the Labrador is by far the most popular retrieving dog in Great Britain.* (JAMES DOUGLAS)

most likely that some of the Labradors which appeared in their kennels originated from the sea traders, although it is known that they also received dogs into their Scottish stock from the Malmesbury kennel. Other personalities such as the Hon. A. Holland-Hibbert, later to become Lord Knutsford, did much to establish the breed, and of course the Royal Family took numbers of the breed into their kennels. Such an accolade, combined with the brilliance of their work, assured the breed's future.

However, no mention of the breed can ever be made without acknowledging the efforts of Lorna, Countess Howe, who probably did more than anyone else to establish the Labrador. It was she who founded the first breed club, and she is largely responsible for the compilation and setting down of the breed standard.

The Labrador is probably the dog that holds the distinction of being used as a water dog for the longest period of time, for he was the master of the cold, wild waters of the region in which he developed – the communities around Newfoundland – communities that made much of their living from the seas and river estuaries.

The Labrador was used as a general factotum on the fishing boats when they set out to long line the cod. It was the Labrador who was trained to pick up ropes that had fallen over the side, to take messages from one boat to another, or, holding a plug of wood attached to a leader rope, swim to the shore to the waiting fishermen after the net had been laid. The technique was a good one. By laying the net in a parallel line to the shore and by sending a dog swimming in with the leader, it saved much effort on the part of the boatmen!

The Labrador was also the principal dog of the market gunners, although in areas where the Chesapeake Bay Retriever was more popular, he was used to a lesser extent. Before the advent of the deep freeze or factory farming, large numbers of coastal inhabitants would shoot wildfowl commercially to service the markets throughout the population centres of the Eastern Seaboard, and this was the activity where the dog was to prove his greatest service. Possessed of great stamina, with bulky shoulders, dense waterproof coat and superb marketing ability, they would enter the water repeatedly as they retrieved bird after bird. A hundred retrieves a day was not unusual, with some really superior animals reputed to have retrieved up to two hundred birds in one day. They also had the remarkable capacity of being able to mark up to six birds down at a time.

Today the Labrador is still by far the most popular retriever of the gundog breeds, not only as a working dog, but also on the show bench, and this has resulted in two distinct and separate categories of Labradors. The dogs bred for the showbench have their emphasis put on looks alone, and although there are a few owners who also train their dogs for the gun, the majority of showdogs are never used for any form of fieldsports. At the other end of the scale are the trialling dogs. Field trialling has developed into a highly competitive sport, with large sums of money to be earned from stud fees of a Field Trial Champion, and as it has become more competitive, greater emphasis has been put on the dog's speed and mental capabilities.

This has resulted in strains of trialling dogs progressively getting further away from the standard of the breed, with some highly qualified trialling dogs that have reached Field Trial Champion status – with their snipey, pointed heads, curly tails and narrow shoulders – bearing little resemblance to the traditional Labrador. Although many of these dogs may be excellent in the field, they would not survive particularly well if they were to be transported back to compete in work with their forebears.

It is, however, entirely possible to find Labradors that do conform to the physical attributes desirable in the standard, whilst at the same time having impeccable trialling and working blood in their veins.

For the man who wants a malleable (relatively), easily trained and maintained dog, the Labrador is the obvious choice, for he – more than any other dog in the shooting field – is the supreme retriever, whether he is required to battle through icy seas during a coastal fowling trip, or merely to pick a pheasant from a root field. But it is when the pheasant has run off, doing his best to hide and avoid capture, that the Labrador's scenting powers prove his supremacy and few birds can successfully give an experienced Labrador the slip.

Then again, the potential dog buyer must ask himself what type of shooting he is intending to do. Many people believe that the Labrador is not a hunting dog. This 'myth' has come about because Labradors are never asked to 'hunt' in trialling situations. All dogs are capable of hunting, some merely do it better than others. For the sportsman who puts greater emphasis on retrieving – but wants a dog that will quarter in front of him (albeit not as successfully and not with as much flair as either a spaniel or a pointer) – then a Labrador is an entirely acceptable choice.

## Flat-coated Retriever

Probably the prettiest, and certainly the most elegant looking of all the retrievers is the Flat-coat, and at one time, during the period around the early 1900s, he was the natural choice for the fashionable shooting man.

It is difficult to know quite how much work or planning was put into the development of the breed, but it must have been considerable. Mr S. E. Shirley of Ettington (1844–1904) who also has the distinction of being the founder of the Kennel Club, originated the modern Flat-coat during the 1860s in England, initially from the combination of breeding together Labradors and Newfoundlands, both specialist water dogs from the north-eastern coast of the American continent. Originally the breed was known as the wavy-coated retriever, but although the dog was reputed to be an excellent worker, his bulky, heavy coat was found to cause him unnecessary effort in the water, restricting the amount of work he could do because much of his energy was spent in propelling himself. As a result, the heavy bulky coat was gradually bred out of the breed until he became known as the Flat-coated Retriever.

To look at one of these dogs, with their elegant lines, aristocratic carriage and general flair, it is easy to see the influence of both Irish and Gordon Setters, and possibly even Pointer, who are all credited with being introduced to the breed to achieve their fine looks.

Before the Labrador came to real prominence, the Flat-coat was regarded as the gentleman's shooting dog, but the Labrador, who generally displayed greater speed and agility coupled with superior water work, pushed the Flat-coat into second place.

In the working field the Flat-coat is truly excellent, and there is little to choose between a good Flat-coat and a Labrador, so it is difficult to understand why the dog should ever have fallen from popularity. It is probably due to simple taste and fashion change, and – as is common in so many field sports matters – the public tend to follow current trends. But he is truly an excellent dog, and the shooting man who likes his looks and wants to be a little different, could certainly buy one of these dogs with confidence, if he can find a dog of proven working ancestry.

Sadly the Flat-coat is popular as a show dog, because of his fine looks and even temperament, which it makes it difficult to find true working dogs. Another sad fact about this delightful breed is that although some are run in trials, they are largely in amateur hands, so the breed is seldom given an opportunity to really show its worth.

## Golden Retriever

Although a popular retrieving breed, the Golden Retriever has largely gone to the show bench, mainly because of its beautiful golden coat, gentle nature and kind disposition. There are, however, still many goldies used in the shooting field.

*The Flat-coat Retriever, once the preferred breed, has fallen behind the Labrador in popularity as a gundog. This wonderful photograph shows the breed in its heyday.*

*Golden Retriever being sent for a retrieve, watched by the rest of the training class.* (JAMES DOUGLAS)

The breed originated at the kennel of Lord Tweedmouth who had purchased a wavy-coated retriever and which in 1868 he used to service a bitch of local breeding referred to as a Tweed water spaniel. The issue of this union was Primrose, Ada, Cowslip and Crocus. From these four animals the Golden Retriever of today has its origins. Although generally not fast or powerful with water work, some goldies can be excellent in this environment, though it must be said that since they have a tendency to swim lower in the water – because of their heavy, long coats – they would not be the ideal choice for a wildfowler.

If obtained from proven working stock they can be a rewarding dog to work with, and the field sportsman who shoots in an environment suitable for this breed can approach the Golden Retriever with confidence.

The breed generally reaches maturity later than other retrieving breeds. However, for the modern shooting man who does not enjoy the luxury of kennelling his dog, it can be inconvenient to have such a long-haired animal. To keep it looking its best and to maintain a healthy coat can be time consuming, as it is prone to picking up and retaining dirt and burrs more readily than one of its shorter-haired cousins.

## Curly-coated Retriever

For the man who is prepared to put a lot of work and devotion into his dog, who is able to keep him with him, preferably in the house (at least for part of the time), who wants a dog with individuality, a dog that is not for the social shooter standing at a peg, but more for the true wildfowler, then there is no better choice than the Curly-coated Retriever. This big, tough, strong dog is without doubt the best of the retrievers for the true widlfowler who is able to train and handle this rewarding breed.

The largest and most individual of the retrievers, the curly is probably the result of the cross-breeding of the Standard Poodle, the Irish Water Spaniel and the Labrador, and first appeared in England in the nineteenth century. It is strange that such a potentially fabulous water dog has never become more popular with the many rough shooters and fowlers. But this is probably in part due to fashion – he is not as demonstrative as a Golden Retriever, or as elegantly good looking as a Flat-coat. He is not as quick as the Labrador, neither is he as easily trained.

It is in his training that he is probably most demanding, since Curly-coateds generally require more knowledgeable handling. A Labrador, for instance, is more forgiving if the handler makes mistakes – not so the curly. He is slow to mature and is not really fully developed into complete adulthood until he is three years old, and, because of his individuality, is not so easily trained. The only way I know of really making a success of a curly is to get to know him really well, to understand how he thinks, to appreciate how he works out a problem, to work together with him, to be the essence of patience, and to combine firmness with sensible handling. With luck, at the end of the day the curly will be the sort of gundog you will be proud to shoot with.

The most distinctive feature of this dog is of course the coat, which is made up of tiny tight curls of dense hair, so tightly packed that the coat is not only impenetrable to any form of comb or brush, but provides a perfect protection from the most daunting of cover, which the curly will happily push through if required. The coat is the very essence of water repellence. It also traps a thin layer of air when the dog enters water, which acts as insulation from the cold. A small bonus with the coat is that the air trapped also gives extra buoyancy to the dog when swimming. Because of his temperament the curly is also more a one-man dog than any of the other

*Curly-coated Retriever: the largest and most individual of the retrieving breeds.* (JAMES DOUGLAS)

retrievers. He will identify with his home more than other breeds and, in consequence, is an excellent watchdog.

One seldom sees curlys at shows and they have never caught the public imagination as much as the other more showy, gentle and good-looking retrievers.

## Pointers and Setters

### English Setter

Setters were used by sportsmen long before the development of game shooting as a sport. They worked then as they do now, finding game and flushing it, but in those days it would be flown down by falcons or coursed by greyhounds rather than shot. They were also used by hunters netting coveys of young grouse or partridge: the dogs' 'setting' or crouching attitude when on point allowing the hunters to drag a net right over the dog and the birds alike. As better and more reliable guns were developed the sport of shooting birds on the wing became fashionable and hunters began to shoot game over their dogs as well as using hounds and falcons to pursue it or nets to entangle it.

English Setters are elegant, athletic hunting dogs with a long, feathery coat in a mixture of white with black, lemon, orange or tan ticking or patches. During the nineteenth century there were many different strains of setter in England, often distinguished by the name of the breeder, but around 1870 the Kennel Club elected to lump them all together as 'English Setters'. Two of the best known strains were those developed by Edward Laverack and later by Purcell Llewellin, and some breeders still employ those sub-classifications to the present day and talk of 'Laverack' and 'Llewellin' setters as if they were separate breeds.

As with all pointers and setters the English Setter is characterized by his pace, stamina and style, particularly when seen working in his natural environment on a grouse moor. When pointing, or 'setting', they tend to adopt a stance with head and tail raised so as to produce an elegant curved top line. The breed has a reputation for being sticky on point but there are plenty of working English Setters that will rode in to their birds as freely as any of the other pointing breeds. Sensitive by nature, they require sympathetic handling and training, but are capable of working long, hard days on the hill.

*The noble head of a handsome working English Setter.* (DAVID HUDSON)

The divide between the show and working strains is probably wider in English Setters than with almost any other breed. The show setter is typically a big, handsome dog with long feathering and beautiful, but empty, head and a complete lack of the drive needed to work for the gun. If you want an English Setter to work though there are plenty of well-established working lines available for the owner who takes the time to seek them out.

## Irish Setter

The Irish Setter or Red Setter is by far the most popular of the pointing breeds in terms of numbers registered annually at the Kennel Club but the great majority of those dogs are show or pet dogs rather than working dogs. There are still plenty of good, working strains of Irish Setter though and there should be no difficulty in finding one from working lines for anyone who wants a red dog to shoot over. The original Irish Setters were red and white rather than the solid red colour that is so familiar today, and over the last twenty years or so the red and white strain has begun to re-appear at shows and trials. The numbers of red and white Irish Setters are comparatively low at the moment but they are certainly handsome dogs with the contrast of white and the typical Irish Setter rich chestnut colouring in their coats. They also have the advantage of being easier to spot when they are setting birds against the heather than the solid red dogs that can blend in to the background, particularly on dull days.

Irish Setters are typically friendly, bouncy, rollicking dogs with a fun-loving attitude towards life and work alike. They have great stamina and seem largely impervious to cold, wet or heat when at work. They are sometimes slow to mature and their sense of fun can make training and working them something of an adventure. They are generally very affectionate, which accounts in part for their popularity as pet dogs, though the boundless energy of a working bred Irish Setter means that it needs a lot of exercise to keep it out of mischief. The show and pet strains tend to be less energetic: an advantage to the pet owner but not to the sportsman who wants his dog to run many hard miles in the course of a day's shooting.

The breed has developed a reputation for being wild and difficult to train but this is largely due to their popularity as pets bringing them into the

*Keen interest is shown by this working Irish Setter.* (DAVID HUDSON)

*This Gordon Setter is well suited to the harsh weather of the Scottish grouse moors.* (DAVID HUDSON)

hands of owners who do not have the time, the patience or the ability to train and exercise them properly.

### Gordon Setter

The third of the British setters is the Gordon: an exceptionally handsome dog with a predominantly black coat set off by tan markings on the paws, chest, muzzle and eyebrows. They are named after the Duke of Richmond and Gordon who maintained a kennel of setters at Gordon Castle in the early nineteenth century, though black coloured setters had been around long before that. Like the Irish Setter, the Gordon Setter once had white markings though anything more that a trace of white is now considered unacceptable.

The Gordon is a slightly heavier dog than either the English or Irish Setter and tends to work at a slightly slower pace, though this should be set off by exceptional stamina. Tough, hardy dogs they are well suited to the cold, wet weather sometimes associated with their native country. Less gregarious than the Irish Setter they often turn into 'one man dogs', with eyes only for their owners. The difference in pace between the Gordon Setter and the other native setter is probably less marked now than in the past, and certainly on the field trial circuit the Gordons can usually match, if not beat, the other runners for speed. In the shooting field, where pace is less important, their stamina and excellent noses hold them in good stead.

## The Pointer

The Pointer (often, but incorrectly called the English Pointer) is the fourth of the native British birddogs, though like the others his ancestors probably came to Britain from continental Europe. The forebear of the modern Pointer is generally accepted as the Spanish Pointer: a much heavier and slower dog, probably introduced to these shores by soldiers returning from the War of the Spanish Succession around 1713. Breeders introduced a variety of blood lines including foxhound, greyhound and bloodhound in order to produce a lighter, faster dog that retained the staunchness on point of the old Spanish Pointer and by the turn of the eighteenth century they were shooting over Pointers that look exactly like those we know today.

The modern Pointer is a lean, athletic dog with the ability to run fast and effortlessly over moorland or stubbles. Like the setters he has a superb nose that can detect the presence of a single grouse crouched in the heather fifty yards away even though he is running at top speed. Pointers have a short, springy coat, quite different from the long feathered coats of the setters and are usually a combination of white with black, liver, orange or lemon markings, though whole coloured black pointers are not unknown. The short coat is said by some observers to make them more suitable than setters for work on the moors during the heat of August, while rendering them more susceptible to cold, wet conditions. While most setters seem to take hot days in their stride it is certainly true that some Pointers detest cold and wet conditions, particularly when they are walking on their leads rather than hunting.

There are probably more working Pointers in the country than any of the setter breeds, though the Irish Setter is far more common if show and pet homes are counted. Although there is a clear divide between show lines and working bred dogs the gap is less marked in Pointers than in most of the other gundog breeds and in recent years a Pointer has achieved dual Champion status by becoming both a Field Trial Champion and a Show Champion. Even so, if you are seeking a Pointer pup for a shooting dog it is still best to select one from proven working stock.

*The Pointer was once the first choice of the shooting man when the partridge season opened.* (DAVID HUDSON)

## Hunting, Pointing, Retrieving Breeds (HPRs)

### German Short-haired Pointer

Dog owners have very individual taste when it comes to a dog's looks. Some people who are 'spaniel' men can see little to admire in an HPR dog, finding them not to their taste. Yet to others the HPRs are the epitome of grace and beauty.

The German Short-haired Pointer (GSP) is undoubtedly the most popular of the HPR dogs in Britain today, and they have, over the last few years, gained an increasing number of enthusiasts who have taken this breed very much to heart, captivated by his sheer versatility in the field and his good looks. Whilst it is a pleasure to watch any working dog as he carries out the tasks he has been trained for – the Springer bustling through cover or the Labrador doing a long distance retrieve on a difficult run – it is the excellence with which some of these dogs carry out the job that appears and attracts, not necessarily the dog's physical good looks. This is not the case with the HPR dogs, and the GSP in particular, for to the enthusiast of the breed they have the added bonus of being physically pleasing to the eye as they work. With their short coats and well-muscled configuration they display a grace and athleticism in some ways almost feline.

The forerunners of the GPS began in the seventeenth century, with the combination of the Spanish pointer and schweisshund. The pointer gave the strain the ability to point game and the schweisshund (a track hound not dissimilar to our own bloodhound) introduced the ability to follow scent. This was the basis of the German pointer. A later introduction of the 'English-style'

*A young liver and white German Short-haired Pointer.* (JAMES DOUGLAS)

pointer gave the breed a lighter, more streamlined and generally faster influence, with the additional input of retriever and foxhound blood. It is from these origins that the GSP evolved. This has resulted in the dogs of today having the best attributes of the specialists – the retrieving ability of the retriever, the persistence on a scent of the bloodhound, the pointing characteristics of the pointer and the keen hunting instincts of the foxhound.

The GSP is ideally suited to the man who shoots on his own or in the company of one or two friends. He is not suitable for the man who walks game in the company of several others, since he must range widely on either side of the gun and is likely to go on point further down the line. This gives the gun the immediate problem of who shoots the bird – the man who the dog is pointing in front of (and who by rights should have the game) – or should the handler break line and go to the dog?

Neither is the GSP suitable as a peg dog with the formality of steady and controlled retrieving. To use a GSP for any one of his multiple abilities alone would be unwise – and a waste – for the specialist retrievers or spaniels will do these tasks with greater efficiency. Where the GSP comes into his own is when he is used with all his functions coming into play, and for the rough shooter who wants one dog with the abilities of many, the GSP is an excellent choice.

## Large Munsterlander

The first Large Munsterlander was imported into Britain as recently as 1971, yet this interesting dog cannot be ignored in any discussion on pointer retrievers. Although a recent addition to the British gundog scene, the Munsterlander has been well used in Germany for as long as most of their other gundog breeds. In fact, it is dogs similar to the Munsterlander that appear so often in many old paintings depicting hunting scenes in Germany, although they are often either brown and white, black and white or tri-coloured.

Before the nineteenth century, hunting dogs were judged purely by their ability, and it made good sense to put together the best dogs and bitches, irrespective of colouration. But in the early nineteenth century hunting dog owners and enthusiasts became more conscious of both colour and physical standards, establishing records which recorded which dogs had been bred with each other and the results of the mating. In the case of the Large Munsterlander fashion dictated that the darker colours were more desirable and that the lighter coloured pups should be culled at birth. The breed at that time was regarded as a Long-haired German Pointer.

With the foundation of the German Kennel Club and the establishment of a general studbook, only brown and white Long-Haired German Pointers were permitted to be registered. Any black and white dogs were disallowed, and since they had little value they were discarded – passed on to the grateful hands of the local jagers, foresters and farmers. They had less concern for fashion or officialdom, and no doubt rejoiced at this source of quality dogs, rejected for the seemingly trivial reason of colour alone. So there survived in the Munster region of Germany a whole population of black and white working dogs. It is, of course, from this area that the breed takes its name.

It was not until 1919 with the formation of a club to try to bring all the specimens together officially, and establish a distinct breed, that the Munsterlander was officially recognized and given the name of Black and White Large Munsterlander. I have seen Munsterlanders working in a variety of cover conditions and terrain and they well deserve their reputation as being excellent and worthwhile dogs.

*The handsome russet gold coat is typical of the Hungarian Vizsla.* (JAMES DOUGLAS)

## Hungarian Vizsla

Although the Vizsla is thought of as a Hungarian dog, it has its origins further to the east. The word 'viszla' is Turkish, meaning 'sleek'. They are also sometimes referred to as the Magyar, which bears reference to the invading eastern warriors. One must remember that much of Europe was settled originally from the east, and many dogs were brought with these eastern invaders. The Turks, who occupied Hungary for a large part of the sixteenth and seventeenth centuries are credited with having introduced the pointer-type dog, which was yellow in colour, and it is likely that it was crossed with the local hound, the copo, to form the main ancestry of the Viszla.

It was during the period of the Austro-Hungarian Empire, when the nobility, like the nobility of other European countries, concentrated greatly on the sport of hunting and vast tracts of land were made over to this sport. With game of all types available – including boar, wolves, deer, ground game and wildfowl – these dogs really came into prominence, being bred in kennels owned by the nobility. The Viszla is basically the Hungarian equivalent of the GSP, with slightly different attributes to accommodate the terrain of its origins.

The Viszla falls into the category of being an excellent HPR dog and is generally steadier and quieter than the Weimaraner. They are not common and it is not easy to find one from impeccable working stock.

## Weimaraner

Probably the most distinctive and immediately noticeable point about the Weimaraner is his unusual colour, which ranges from a delicate silvery grey to a dark browny grey. So distinctive is his coat that he has been christened the 'grey ghost' or 'silver ghost' in some parts of America.

With his origins firmly fixed in the noble houses of Germany, the dog has a long and distinguished history in that country. It is difficult to pin down with any certainty the various breeds from which he has evolved, but several theories have been suggested. In seventeenth

*The Weimaraner is a striking dog, sometimes known as the 'Grey Ghost'.* (JAMES DOUGLAS)

century German hunting paintings, dogs are often shown with the same short-haired colouration, and may reflect a purity unbroken since then. It is also suggested that the breed has evolved from cross-breeding hounds and pointers – like the GSP – from which he differs not only in size (being larger) but also in his hunting instincts. He has a tendency to be more hound-like, holding his head lower and using a combination of air and ground scent to find his quarry.

The Weimaraner tends to be more aggressive than the GSP, with a very strong guarding instinct for both his home and family. He is more a dog for the enthusiast of the breed, rather than one of the mainstream HPR owners who would probably be better advised to gravitate towards a GSP.

### German Wire-haired Pointer

The German Wire-haired Pointer is now the most popular shooting dog in Germany and is a breed derived from the short-haired version. But the inclusion of the coarser-haired breeds has produced the thick, hard wiry coat which gives the dog greater protection in cover and keeps him warmer in cold weather. The GWP is becoming increasingly popular in Britain, but numerically it is far behind the much more popular GSP. Their care and training are identical.

### The Brittany

The Brittany was originally known as the Brittany Spaniel when it was first introduced to Britain in the 1980s but the Kennel Club agreed to change the name to just Brittany because the dogs were classed with the Hunt, Point and Retrieve breeds rather than the spaniels. Nevertheless, the Brittany quite clearly is a spaniel, albeit a spaniel that points rather than flushes game. They originate from Brittany in France and were developed by crossing setters brought across from England by sportsmen in the nineteenth century with the local French spaniels. This produced a wide ranging dog, a little longer on the leg than most spaniel types, with an excellent nose and the ability to point game.

The Brittany is a lively, headstrong little dog that shows all the hallmarks of both its spaniel and setter ancestors. As pointing dogs they can range much more widely than flushing spaniels and

*The thick, rough coat of this German Wire-haired Pointer protects him in cover and helps insulate him against the cold.* (DAVID HUDSON)

have both the legs and the drive to do just that. Their energy and enthusiasm can make them quite a handful to train and control in the shooting field, but their ability to combine the pointing instinct with the courage to bash through cover makes them ideal for the man who enjoys a variety of shooting. Equally at home on the open moor or hunting out cover on a rough shoot, the Brittany is deservedly one of the most popular gundogs in France and well established in America.

Brittany enthusiasts in Britain, as with most of the HPR breeds, have endeavoured to ensure that the dogs' working ability is not lost by breeding solely for show points and though they are still not common it should not be difficult for potential owners to find a dog from working lines. They are not the easiest of dogs to handle and are probably not a good choice for the novice. They need a lot of exercise and plenty of mental stimulation to keep them out of trouble.

## Italian Spinone

The Italian Spinone, like the Brittany, was introduced to Britain in the early 1980s, though in many ways they are at opposite ends of the HPR spectrum. The Spinone is a big, heavy dog weighing up to eighty pounds and has a thick, wiry coat with bristling eyebrows and a shaggy beard and moustache. This heavy coat makes them impervious to cold and wet and also provides protection when they are working in thick and thorny cover. Their colour is predominantly white with orange or brown markings and they are generally quiet, friendly dogs.

Unlike the other HPR breeds the Spinone works at a fast trot rather than at a gallop, but they can cover a lot of ground in the course of a day and their easy pace means they will work for hours on end and miss very little game. Allied to their steady pace is an equable temperament that makes them easier to train and handle than some of the more excitable Hunt, Point and Retrieve breeds. They are good retrievers and work well in boggy or marshy ground as well in thicker cover, though their lack of pace would probably put them at a disadvantage on the open hill where game can be very scarce.

# 4
# CHOOSING YOUR PUPPY

Once you have decided which particular breed is going to best suit your type of sport, think also about your domestic situation. Can the dog be kennelled, do you live in a flat, are you out at work all day or can someone be at home with the puppy? These factors should, of course, be taken into account when deciding on the size of the breed you choose and the age it is best to have the puppy. If you live in a flat there is little point in having a great bounding GSP or Curly-coat when a smaller breed would be less obtrusive and fit in better to your environment. If someone is going to be with the dog all day, then you could consider a small puppy since it is easier to house-train a puppy if he can be watched at all times.

Having made your decision you must remember one important fact which is applicable to all aspects of gundog training, from the time of choosing the puppy right through to the end of his training. **You are not in a race**. If you buy or train in haste then you will have years of leisure to regret your urgency.

When buying a puppy be prepared to cast your net as wide as possible. The columns of the shooting press normally contain plenty of advertisements for quality puppies of all recognized breeds, and while it may be more convenient to buy locally, be prepared to travel whatever distance is necessary to get the right animal.

Normally 'gundog for sale' ads will say that the puppy has been sired by a Field Trial Champion (FTCh), and the dam is either a good working bitch or is out of champion stock. Do not consider buying a dog from any other than proven working stock. Whilst there are many good dogs that never see a trial – and can be wonderful workers – the only true indication that the animal is capable of achieving a good working standard (unless you personally know the owner of both dog and bitch, and have seen them working) is the distinction of the parentage denoted by the field trials awards.

The best time of year to choose a puppy is in the spring, since it gives you the summer months, when the weather is kinder, to let the pup grow out of babyhood, and avoiding the cold when it is unpleasant for both you and the dog to be outside regularly. There is also the additional problem of the puppy being more susceptible to winter chills and using up vital bodybuilding protein just keeping itself warm.

The first question I am often asked is which sex to have and what are the advantages or disadvantage of male and female dogs. Quite simply there is no difference whatever in their ability to work, although dogs are generally stronger and may have a tendency to be stronger-willed. However, dogs do not come into season, with the inconvenience that this brings. A dog, if made up to a Champion, can be used for stud, though this is a very small (and unlikely) consideration for the average shooter. Basically a dog is simply a larger and stronger version of the bitch, able to work twelve months of the year in company.

*These Cocker Spaniels at a field trial are certain to be bred from proven working stock.* (DAVID HUDSON)

Bitches of course come into season, and during this period they are attractive to any dog, which eliminates any chance of you shooting in the company of others who may own dogs. On the other hand, you can take puppies from a bitch in later years, and if you have any intention of ever doing so then the choice is made. Bitches have a tendency to be mellower in temperament and generally content themselves better to a domestic situation. Lastly, personal preference is the final consideration when making the choice as to sex. Some dog owners have a preference for one sex or the other. But when it comes down to pure training and workability, there is no difference.

When you arrive at a kennel to buy a puppy, before you bother to look at the pups – and perhaps be influenced by several appealing round and cuddly little bodies, ask if it is possible to see the sire. If a stud dog has been used, then it would not normally be possible, but the next question you should ask is to see the pups' pedigree. There you should find the prefix 'FTCh' in front of several of its forebears.

The pedigree of the litter is extremely important to the potential gundog owner, and a short explanation of the various facets of this often confusing certificate is appropriate. As I have said, unless you know the parents of the puppies personally, the only indicator that they will be of any use as working dogs is the number of Field Trials Champions and – to a less extent – Field Trials Winners to be found in the pedigree.

Although the pedigree normally goes back several generations, the most important generations are the first three from the left – parent, grandparents and great-grandparents. If there are Field Trials Champions in any of these generations, hopefully – though not necessarily – on both sides of the pedigree (that is, in the ancestry of both the sire and the dam), you can be reasonably sure that your new dog has the potential to become an excellent gundog. Both the sire and the dam's line should have proven working dogs in evidence at some point. When looking for Field Trials dogs in the pedigree be careful of two things. The letters 'FTW' can sometimes – quite incorrectly – be used to denote a Field Test Winner. If the breeder is reputable this should not be a problem, but if in doubt ask. The other prefix to look out for is the simple 'Ch'. This means that the dog is a Champion, but has nothing to do with working ability and denotes a Show Champion (more frequently shown as 'ShCh'). Once again, if in doubt, ask the breeder.

I have often heard it said that a dog with any show blood in its ancestry should be rejected without question. I do not subscribe to that policy for two reasons. Firstly, I prefer my dogs to be physically attractive and to look as the breed should. Secondly, as long as the show blood is three or more generations removed from the puppy I cannot see how it could adversely affect the working ability of the dog. Indeed it is likely that the show blood was purposefully added to the line to improve the physical appearance of the progeny.

Once you have satisfied yourself that the pedigree is in order, ask to see the puppies. Carefully observe the conditions in which the puppies are kept. If you are taken into the garden shed, and there in the corner is a puppy box covered with excrement and urine, giving you a general feel of poor standards, then this could also give you an indication of what sort of person the breeder is. If, on the other hand, the puppies are kept in clean, warm surroundings, with only fresh excrement visible (a litter of growing puppies can produce a large volume of excrement in a few hours) this would normally indicate that the breeder has higher standards.

Looking at the puppies, irrespective of how wonderful they seem, has little bearing on the eventual size and physical appearance of the adult dog. Labrador puppies, for instance, with their round ball heads, short coupled bodies and little short, thick otter tails, can, in a few months of growth, change their shape entirely. The round ball head can stretch out into a snipe-like and undesirable line and the little tail can miraculously grow and curl. So – as in humans – the only true guide you will have as to the pups' appearance in adulthood is from the parents.

When you are looking at a young puppy open its mouth and check that it has a correct scissor bite, making sure that when the mouth is closed, the teeth of the lower jaw fit neatly behind the teeth of the upper jaw. If there is an undue space between the teeth the dog would be overshot. If, on the other hand, the teeth of the lower jaw protrude beyond the teeth of the upper jaw, the dog would be undershot. Both of these faults are genetic and must be avoided.

Look at the pup's eyes. Are they the dark standard that the breed requires, or are they light in colour? A light coloured eye should also be avoided. A puppy's legs should be thick, strong and

*The correct way to hold a small puppy with your hand supporting its chest.* (JAMES DOUGLAS)

straight. Feet splayed out, bowlegs, or any distortion should be left alone.

With all puppies the benchmark should be that if it is bright and alert – and a smaller, plumper version of its parents – with good strong limb bones, then it is a well set up little puppy. If you just cannot make up your mind and find yourself in doubt, then it is as well to take someone with you who is more experienced in choosing puppies.

There are many silly ideas as to the correct way of choosing which puppy from a litter, such as sending your child to get it, or sticking your hand into the litter box with eyes closed, taking the first pup you feel! These strange notions stem from the fact that it can sometimes be extremely difficult to find one puppy that stands out from the litter. However, since owning a gundog is a highly personal thing, it is infinitely preferable that you make an informed choice , choosing an animal you like right from the outset – one that appeals to *you*.

The best way of doing this is to watch the puppies. Stick your hand in and see which ones are least afraid of you. Is there one that comes in curiously towards your hand? Is there one that hides in the corner, appearing timid and afraid? Is there a big bold puppy that stands out cheekily from the rest? That is the one to choose. Avoid the timid beast that is afraid of human contact and go for the bold one.

Make sure you get a copy of the pedigree and Kennel Club registration certificate and put the puppy into your car. It is wise to have taken with you a good stout cardboard box, liberally carpeted with newspapers, since the pup will almost certainly either soil the box on the journey home, or vomit, or both.

When you get the puppy home, give him time to settle down in his new surroundings. Try to keep the family back from him until he himself comes out looking to see what is going on. Very often this is an anti-climax. You arrive home, having told the family not to crowd around and frighten the pup, and with expectation they watch you carry in the box with the new arrival – supposedly cowering timidly inside. You put it on the floor and this tiny bundle of fun leaps from the box and proceeds to waddle around the floor, curiously investigating everything and giving no sight of his recent journey! Still it is wise to err on the cautious side and assume that the new arrival will be at least a little timid and strange. It is unlikely that he will have seen more than the occasional human face for short periods of time and – up until now – will not have been away from the comfort and warmth of his brothers and sisters, as well as his mother. All of a sudden his world has changed – bright lights, different smells and possibly several loud and excited children, all clamouring to look, touch and hug this wonderful new member of the family. So let him investigate you and your family in his own time.

After he has settled down, it is best to give him a warm meal and bed him down for the night. You will of course have prepared for the new arrival, either by having prepared the kennel where he is to live, or if he is to be kept in the house, a bed in a box, on an uncarpeted floor where any overnight soiling can be easily cleaned.

For the first few nights when a young puppy is away from the nest for the first time he is likely to yodel and yap, howling for attention. You should understand that this howling is temporary and has to be endured. He will soon realize that if his howling gets no response, and does not result in you coming to see him, it is a pointless exercise, and the howling will stop. There are, however, a number of things you can do to help give him comfort, and make the howling less persistent.

Firstly, and most important, any baby or young creature sleeps better on a full stomach. So if you give a puppy a good meal not more than an hour before you want him to bed down for the night, he will not only have moved his bowels quickly after being fed, but be prepared for bed. The sensations that have been taken away from him are a heat source from his brothers and sisters, his mother (although by the time the pups are ready to leave the nest the mother will no longer have much contact with them), and the general 'puppy' noise. You can do something to simulate these sensations and give him comfort as he settles into your home. This is particularly advisable with a young puppy that is a determined and loud howler – especially if you have neighbours!

An old-fashioned alarm clock, put out of his reach, will give a ticking sound. If you don't possess such a clock then a radio – playing quietly – will do. For the heat source an old-fashioned stone hot-water bottle is ideal. Pad it well by pushing it inside a couple of thick socks or wrap it in an old towel and tie it up. The idea is to give him a chew-proof heat source, simulating the warmth and comfort of his mother. A standard hot-water bottle will not do as he may well burst it. If you cannot procure a stone bottle into which he can cuddle, then try to keep him in a warm environment. This is only a temporary situation, but if you can provide warmth, and a little background noise it will give him comfort, and give you more chance of an undisturbed night's sleep.

A young puppy not only represents the beginnings of what is going to be your dream of a perfect gundog of the future, he also represents an appealing plaything. It is therefore important that you 'dog train' your family by explaining to them that the dog will gain nothing by being endlessly poked, prodded, cuddled and fed sweets. It is also potentially dangerous for puppies to be lifted by inexperienced hands, as this can put tremendous strain on its internal organs and if dropped its young, soft bones and muscles can be damaged by the fall.

The correct way to lift a puppy is to completely support its stomach. This is best done by passing your arm between his hind legs, with your fingers splayed on his chest. This means the dog is fully supported for the entire length of his body, with only his four legs dangling on either side of your arm. Another method of lifting a puppy is with one hand supporting the stomach and the other supporting the chest.

Of course all puppies and young dogs, particularly those being kept indoors, benefit from human contact and playing with children, but this must be kept to a happy medium. Another danger area with a small appealing puppy is to allow him up on chairs beside you. This is humanizing the dog. How is the puppy to know why, as he gets older and larger – and having got into the habit as a baby of being allowed on the furniture – you suddenly change the rules, and this is no longer allowed? If you have small children, it is well to remember that puppies can house parasites, and small fingers can transfer a variety of nasty bacteria into small mouths and eyes.

Being a family dog as well as a gundog is perfectly acceptable, but it does not mean that your new dog must enjoy the same standards and facilities as your children. He is after all a dog, and if kept in his place from puppyhood, many of the problems of later years can be avoided.

# 5
# EARLY TRAINING

There is no magic day in the calendar when your dog should start his training. Some dogs are steadier, quieter and give the impression of being keen to learn earlier than others. Most dogs should be able to start their early training between six and seven months, whilst others may not be ready until they are older.

## Building the foundations

Throughout all gundog training every task, lesson or command you give to your dog hinges on one foundation stone – discipline. Without your dog being disciplined and under your command and control, you can do nothing. So early discipline training is vital, making him aware of your voice and introducing him to the pleasures of working with you. Without working continually on these very basic discipline exercises you will allow your young dog to develop bad habits, and like all habits, they can be very difficult to eradicate. Most faults found in adult dogs can be traced back to shoddy discipline work in the early formative months of training. So *at all times* you must be in control of the dog and never let him forget that.

Whilst I maintain that there is no mystique in training a gundog, and that anyone with a modicum of commonsense can turn out a good dog, there is one aspect of working with a young dog that is absolutely vital. It is so important to the future success of a potential gundog, that unless you – the trainer and handler – are able to say with absolute confidence that you have that particular 'something' within yourself, you would be better to send your dog to a professional kennel for training. The ingredient I am referring to is patience. You must never lose your patience when you are training your dog, even if he does not seem to be able to grasp a particular lesson for the moment. Everyone, including dogs, can have off days, and if you feel you are in danger of becoming frustrated and annoyed with your dog it is better to stop your training session and return home. If you try to continue under these circumstances you can do irreversible damage to the 'special' relationship you are trying to build with your dog.

You should never shout at your dog. If he does not obey the command given in a normal tone of voice, there is no reason for him to obey you when you shout at him. Even worse, you are creating a precedent in his mind – if he gets used to the shouted command he will not obey the spoken command. Dogs have excellent hearing, so there is absolutely no reason for you to strain your vocal chords in an effort to make him obey. A quietly spoken but *firm* word is all that is required.

Another aspect of training which I must emphasize at this stage, is to avoid boredom brought on by repetition. Not only will the dog cease to enjoy his work, but he will begin to anticipate your commands. For example, if you always go to the same spot, throw the same dummy in the same place, and send him to retrieve it, you will soon find that before the dummy has left your hand the dog has raced off to the spot where it is expected to land, so that he can bring it back to you. If you make every part of his training simple and fun, you should find few problems with him. Enjoyment is the key to much of his training. All working dogs must enjoy what they are doing, particularly if, as is in the case with gundogs, they are required to use their brains, and to perform for you. If they do not enjoy the tasks put forward for them, they will not do them; it is as simple as that.

By now your dog should be sitting nicely on command. He should sit on the verbal command 'sit' or by hand signal, his response being almost automatic.

When you take your dog out for a training session, whether you live in the country or the city and whether you can walk or must drive to the area where you are going to train your dog, it is important that you let him relieve himself first. If there are rabbits likely to be on your ground, walk them off the area you intend to work your dog before you start. If your young dog spots and then chases a rabbit that is still on the ground, call him back, but under no circumstances chastize him for this. He is young and untrained, and does not yet know that such things are forbidden. If you do beat him you may just be planting the seed in his mind that picking up rabbits equals a beating and he will refuse to pick game at all. Just try and ensure that such occurrences do not happen again.

## Walking to heel

When a small puppy is fitted with a lead it is normally sufficient just to use it as a restraint to keep him with you. But as he gets used to it, you can start to introduce him to the 'heel' command. Personally, I prefer not to start giving this command until the dog is about six months old, using the lead up to this point purely as a way of attaching him to me.

The 'heel' command is simple. Using a gundog rope lead, slip it over the dog's head keeping it slack. Let the dog stray forward, then firmly jerk him back into position as you say the word 'heel'. Normally if this is repeated on two or three occasions the dog quickly learns to pace himself and walk beside you rather than stray forward and get what he knows will be a sharp jerk backwards. Firmness in this particular command will save many later problems, for it is better for your dog to endure three or four hard and sharp jerks rather than numerous gentle ones that he will soon get used to and then ignore.

The alternative way of introducing this command is to carry with you a light switch – such as a twig – and swing it like a pendulum as you walk, so that it passes in front of the dog's face. This will have the natural effect of making him walk in position. Unfortunately it can, with some dogs, create the problem of making him walk out from you, and I wouldn't advocate the use of the switch at this early stage. Better just to jerk him back into position when necessary and make him walk with his head on a level with your knee, or even a pace behind – but not in front of you – since you will shortly be introducing him to sitting when you stop. If his head is in front of you he will be less able to either pace himself to your speed or to see when you stop walking.

When you are quite confident that your dog understands and obeys the 'heel' command you can make him walk to heel without the lead. Because you have always kept him on a slack lead when walking you simply remove the lead from the dog, repeat the word 'heel' and he should walk on beside you as before. From that point on, whenever you take your dog for a walk alternate

*Handler using a rope slip lead to teach this young Labrador to sit and walk to heel.* (JAMES DOUGLAS)

walking with the lead and without it for short periods. Do not be tempted at this stage, however, to try walking without the lead where he is likely to encounter distractions such as people, other dogs, rabbits or other game. Remember he is still a young dog and it is really asking too much of him to expect that level of discipline yet.

## The first training sessions

Put your dog on the lead – and this applies to all breeds – walk him nicely to heel in a zigzag line, whilst you vary the pace at which you walk. This makes the dog aware of your speed and he will vary his speed accordingly. He must pace himself to keep up with you, never the other way around. Take the lead off the dog and continue walking him to heel for a short distance before commanding him to sit. Stand in front of the dog and, with your arm raised in a Nazi-style salute, keep him in the sitting position, and take a few slow paces backwards, always ready to go forward and command him to sit (by gently pushing his hindquarters firmly down into a sitting position as you repeat the command 'sit') if he stands up. If he creeps forward return to him and firmly drag him back to where you had left him. Push his hindquarters down gently but firmly, and say the word 'sit'. Then walk backwards again. On these first few occasions you should be aiming to get no more than about five metres away from him. Stand still, count up to ten slowly and then go back to the dog and, while you keep him sitting, pat his head, gently praising him.

If your dog is walking well to heel at this stage, stand beside him and, patting your left thigh, say his name and walk on with him to heel. If he has not yet walked to heel without the lead, fit it and walk on with him to heel. Walk in a zigzag course, stopping every now and again, always giving him the command to sit when you stop. The idea in this early discipline training is to make the dog aware of his speed being in direct relation to your pace, and to bind him to walking with you, sitting when you stop, and remaining sat until you tell him to heel. In any one training exercise period, you should try to leave him sitting in three separate positions.

For example:

- Walk him to heel; make him sit when you stop; walk a few yards away; return to him and pat your thigh with your left hand and say 'walk on'.
- Walk on with the dog; stop; tell him to sit; stand beside him for a few minutes then pat your thigh, say 'walk on' and walk on with him.
- Stop; tell him to sit and, repeating the word 'sit', walk a few yards away from him.
- Wait for a minute and return to him; pat your thigh, say 'walk on' and walk on.

Keep practising this particular exercise, continually stretching the distance between you and your sitting dog and the time you leave him sitting before you return. Most dogs quickly grasp the routine once they understand what is expected of them.

As I have said previously, all training hinges on your ability to control your dog quietly and gently and to have him – at all times – under your control. You cannot move to any other form of training until the dog will *consistently* sit on command.

It is of the utmost importance that in five out of six times when you leave your dog in the sitting position and walk away from him, that you return to him, and only in one out of six times do you call him to you. Why? When a dog is left in a sitting position he should be content and happy to remain there, not expecting or anticipating the handler to call him. If a dog is left sitting and you walk away – always to return – he will not become anxious and will not be ready to explode into action as soon as you make the slightest sound or smallest movement. On the one in six occasions when you call your dog to you, pat your right thigh with a straight arm, using big arm movements, so the dog gets used to the visual command as you call his name and encourage him to come to you.

## The whistle

Once he sits to the verbal ('sit') and visual (hand-signal) command you can start to add in the whistle. Leaving the dog in a sitting position, walk twenty-five metres away and call him to you. As he is running towards you, give him the verbal command to sit, raising your right arm in the air. He may sit immediately, or more likely he will slow down and come forward a little more hesitantly. Sharply command him to sit. If he keeps coming right up to you before he sits, firmly take him back to where he was when you first told him to sit, make him sit, and repeat the exercise. Once he masters this lesson you should be able to leave him sitting, walk way, call him to you, stop him half way (using voice and arm) then call him to you again, this time right up beside you where you should make a fuss of him for being a good dog.

Now is the time to introduce the whistle. There are many good whistles on the market, but the one I recommend (and use myself) is the simple, inexpensive plastic 210½ whistle. I do not advocate using silent whistles since I like to be able to modulate the tone to my own ear.

With your dog on the lead walk round the training ground. Tell him to sit as you stop, at the same time giving a shortish 'toot' on the whistle, (equivalent to the 'dash' in Morse code). He will sit because he recognized the verbal command, and he should be well used to sitting whenever you stop. At first the whistle command will be just another sound. But very quickly he should come to associate the act of sitting with the sound of the whistle and the whistle will then become a separate command on its own.

It is best, however, at least in the early training of a young dog, when you call him to you and command him to sit, that you use both the hand signal and the whistle command. Do not be timid with your whistle. Give a good loud blast on it. You want to make sure that the dog has a clear understanding of the sound as eventually you will be expecting him to obey the whistle command from a considerable distance, so start the way you will have to continue and do not be afraid to make a noise.

Through many practice sessions, the dog will soon drop at the sound of the whistle, and you will discover that, almost without trying, your dog will be able to sit to all three commands. You can then start adding in variations of the three:

- Try calling him to you and command him to sit to hand and whistle – without the verbal command.
- Once this is successfully accomplished you can then start calling him to you and use the whistle alone to make him stop. In this way, you will continue to build up the dog's versatility with the 'sit' command.

## Returning to the whistle

Up until now your dog will have come to you either at a hand signal – pat of the right thigh, a verbal command (calling his name), or more usually at this stage, a combination of both. He will only have heard the whistle as a command to sit. Once he has become familiar and totally responsive to these commands, you can add in the whistle recall.

This is easily done by leaving the dog sitting, walking away from him and, when you call him to you, pat your thigh and give your whistle several loud short toots (the 'dot' of Morse code). On hearing the whistle the dog may at first slow down or stop, but you must encourage him on, crouching down to make yourself look less imposing to the dog, and he should soon learn the difference between a single whistle command to sit – tooooooot – and the return signal, which is several – toot, toot, toot, toot. When he returns to you always acknowledge the fact that you are happy with him by praising him.

This early basic discipline training can be greatly enhanced if you always remember to vary the commands as much as possible. It is also important never to spend too long in one training session and remember to watch the dog for signs of disinterest or boredom. It is far more beneficial to your dog (and potentially less frustrating for you) if you try to spend half an hour every day, rather than leaving it until the weekend and giving him an intensive one- or two-day training session. That will almost certainly lead both of you to boredom and sloppiness. If there is absolutely no way you can take your dog out during the week, then you will have to make do with weekend training sessions. But even then spend no more than one hour teaching your dog, particularly at this initial stage of his training.

What have you achieved so far:

- You should be able to walk out with your dog at heel – on or off the lead.
- Have him sit when you stop and remain where he is on command.
- Remain seated whilst you walk on, allowing you to get further and further away before (*five out of six times*) you return to him.
- He should dash towards you on a verbal, visual or whistle command.
- He should stop and sit to a verbal, visual or whistle command.

This early discipline, if approached gently, but firmly, is one of the main foundation stones of all your dog's training and general discipline in years to come.

## Retrieving – but keep it controlled

At the same time you can also introduce your dog to retrieving. Again, the right time to start him on retrieving depends very much on the dog and, if you find that when you throw a dummy the dog shows no interest, then it may be best to put the dummy away for another week or two.

After the initial introduction of your dog to the little 'puppy' dummy or tennis ball, you can either buy a lightweight dog-training dummy from any gunshop, or once again, make one up yourself, in scale to the size of your pup. I like to use a paint roller.

When you go out to start the training session with your dog, throw the dummy a few metres in front of him and encourage him to run for it, with the command 'on' or 'fetch' and using an exaggerated arm movement in the direction you have thrown it, as you give the command. It is worthwhile mentioning at this early stage than whenever you throw a dummy for your dog to retrieve, always try to throw it into the wind, getting him used to the awareness of scent, as he goes for it. It will be a while before he stops relying on his eyes and starts educating his nose, but using the wind now will encourage him, and discipline yourself to be aware of wind direction.

When you throw the dummy, with luck your dog will immediately dash out, grab it and run back to you. As he does this, you must give him much praise and make a fuss of him. If he runs off with the dummy, don't worry. Turn and run away from him, calling him to you. If he is reluctant to come to you, squat down – making yourself as small as possible – and encourage him to come, then when he does, make a great fuss of him before gently removing the dummy from his mouth. One retrieve in any training session is sufficient. What is of greater importance is the fact that he picks it up.

When your dog understands that he is expected to retrieve, you can start restraining his behaviour by making him sit for longer and longer periods of time before you allow him to retrieve the dummy.

Tell him to sit and throw the dummy. If he lunges forward eagerly, repeat the sit command, holding on to him if necessary. Count to ten slowly and allow him to retrieve. If the sit command has been well learnt, this should pose no problem and the dog should soon wait for your command to 'fetch' before he dashes after the dummy. However all dogs are different. Some may be able to control themselves easily and be quite happy to sit until told otherwise, whilst other –

*Keep the dog sitting for a few moments before sending him to collect a retrieve.* (JAMES DOUGLAS)

more excitable – dogs should be eased into the exercise more slowly.

When you send your young dog on a retrieve, try to remember to repeat the word 'steady' as he nears the dummy. Although at this stage he should be able to see the dummy, in his later training – particularly with blind retrieves – when he hears his handler say 'steady' once or twice he will know he is in the right area to find the retrieve.

It is of great help to your dog if, when you send him on a blind retrieve, you line him, giving him the line and direction in which he should run. This is easily done if introduced at an early age on visual retrieves.

To do this throw the dummy where the dog can see it, then crouch down beside him, stroke him, and put your arm straight out in a pointing action towards the retrieve, almost as though you were lining the dog up...and then send him out. Practise it over and over. On all retrieves – where you send the dog from a position beside you – get into the habit of squatting down and lining him up. He will then naturally start to take the line of your arm.

When you come to blind retrieves, line directing with be natural. He will, without thinking about it, run straight out the way you point him and, with the experience of having found the seen retrieve, will naturally go straight out in the direction you indicate.

When you have introduced your young dog to the pleasure of retrieving and he has grasped the concept you must now apply the brakes. Being allowed to retrieve will be a privilege for the dog – not a right. Throughout his life the dog must never get the idea that any retrieve, whatever it is, whether a thrown dummy, one shot from a dummy launcher, or a dead bird, is his property, which he can automatically dash after. He must always remain under your command and the easiest way of teaching him this is simply to pick up most of the retrieves yourself.

Leave him sitting, squat beside him and throw the dummy a few metres, telling him to sit as you throw it. Restrain him if he tries to dash after it, tell him to sit, then go forward and pick the dummy yourself. In any training exercise period it is permissible at first to throw three retrieves which you yourself collect, but never more than one in any training period that the dog is allowed to go for. Later, as we advance his training, we will increase the number of retrieves that he

*Practising dropping the dog as he is running towards the handler.* (JAMES DOUGLAS)

*In the early stages of training always try to throw the dummy into the wind to get your dog used to the awareness of scent.* (JAMES DOUGLAS)

collects, but not until his training is more advanced will he get more than two in a session.

You may find when your young dog dashes out and picks up a retrieve that he does so enthusiastically, but is reluctant either to give it up or bring it back. A common problem that many trainers experience is their dog running around them in a wide arc, refusing to come close enough to deliver the dummy. This can be avoided if you stand against a wall or a fence and squat down, until the dog is confident and happy to run back to you with the dummy in his mouth, waiting for you to take it from him.

Never snatch a dummy from the dog's mouth. Put your hand under his chin and hold the dummy in his mouth for a few seconds before gently removing it with the word 'dead'. I like to get my dogs used to holding the retrieve for a short time before I take it from them, saying 'dead' at all times, as the command for them to spit it out. This means that there is never any danger of the dog spitting the retrieve out as soon as he reaches me and before I am ready to take it. How many shooting men have lost runners in this way?

Conversely however, if your dog is so keen that he is reluctant to hold on to the dummy in his willingness to get on to the next exercise, take the dummy from him as soon as he gets back to you. It is far better to make him always give it to hand than to risk him dropping the retrieve on the ground.

Between the ages of six and nine months, with the exception of introduction to water (which I will come to next) you should concentrate on the basic disciplines of sitting to command, coming to you and stopping on command. To prevent boredom, mix this with a thrown retrieve, which you go for five times out of six. Until all these exercises can be done to perfection, there is no point in moving on to any more advanced lessons.

## Water – when and how

Like every other part of your dog's early training, the introduction to water is largely dependent on how much confidence he has in you. A young dog is not

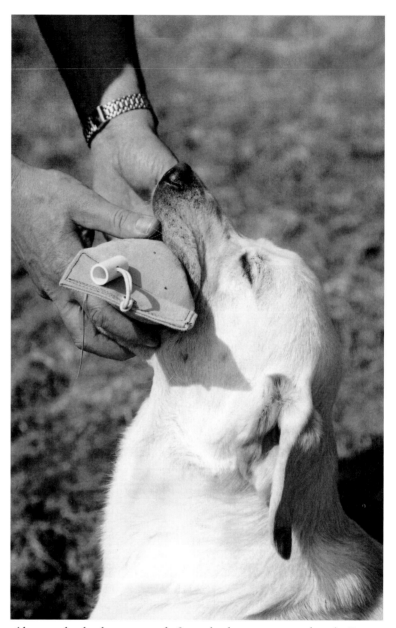

*Always take the dummy gently from the dog; never snatch at it.* (JAMES DOUGLAS)

going to respond to any type of training if he is frightened of you or unsure of your actions. So when you come to introducing him to water you must approach this potentially frightening new environment with great care, on the assumption that he may well be afraid of it. Then, if you

*Encouraging the dog to hold the dummy for a few seconds before gently taking it from him.* (JAMES DOUGLAS)

*Yellow Labrador swimming confidently: but make sure that you give your dog a gentle introduction to water work.* (JAMES DOUGLAS)

discover that he rushes up and dives in without fuss, that is a bonus. But with all young dogs approach this task with the attitude that they are likely to be afraid.

Pick a warm day. If you have access to an older dog who is used to swimming so much the better. With a pair of wellies or waders take your dog to a pond, or slow-moving stream. If there is an older dog with you the pup may follow him into the shallows. It is better, however, for you to go into the water yourself and encourage the young dog in. If he is reluctant, postpone the introduction for another week or so. I have never known any of the retrieving gundog breeds not to enjoy swimming, although some dogs certainly are more reluctant to enter water than others.

Whatever you do you must not force the dog to enter the water, and never be tempted to throw him in. Take time and you will find that a gentle introduction will be much more beneficial in the end. Swimming is after all great fun for most dogs, but – just like humans – they must gain confidence before they can be expected to leap into the water.

# Punishment or reward

There can be no better advice for any gundog owner who wants to get really good results from training his young dog than to establish a loving, happy relationship with the dog during his formative months – his childhood. Play with him as often as you can, take him for walks, indulge him, give him confidence in you. Try never to raise your voice, shout or frighten your young dog, for I have never met any dog of any breed that does not respond well to a loving owner.

By indulgence I do not mean softness. It will be necessary for you to chastize your young dog at different times in his career, but it is best effected by a firm voice. When discipline is needed, intelligence must prevail, for once a dog becomes afraid of you, you are well on your way to losing it. So try to strike a balance and command respect through obedience and affection, rather than chastisement and threats.

The idea of offering a gundog a reward as an aid in training is completely taboo. I would never introduce 'circus type' rewards for tricks performed, but I can see no harm in the rare titbit to help you over a thorny problem. For example, if your young dog, even after many sessions, is unwilling to bring a dummy straight back to you, preferring instead to run about with it in his mouth, then it may be that all he needs is the inducement of a treat to bring him running back to you. A bit of bribery will help you over the hurdle. Once over the hurdle you can put the treats away.

As long as you use the reward method very occasionally you should have no worries with it. If a reward is given too often the dog will become sloppy in his performance because of his keenness to return to you for the expected titbit.

Another advantage in being open to giving your dog a reward is when – for whatever reason – your dog has lost confidence in you. It may be that you unfortunately lost your temper with him, or even another member of the family did, and the dog has become reluctant to come to you. A small treat produced from your pocket can often bring the confidence surging back.

The subject of chastisement is also a difficult one, and must be approached with intelligence and caution. A dog has no memory for crimes committed hours previously. No matter how angry you are at a torn shoe or chewed carpet, any more than showing the dog the crime and a firm 'no' is pointless. You must stop the dog in the act to be effective.

As far as hitting the dog is concerned, a dog taken by the scruff of the neck, shaken, with the word 'no' said firmly, is normally punished sufficiently. For more serious and immediate chastisement, the open palm of your hand is all that is needed, for one must remember that to administer pain to a dog is ineffectual. It is your displeasure, causing fear of you that will bring results.

The whole business of knowing exactly how much punishment to administer often confuses people. A dog was once brought to me to see if I could make any improvements in him. His owner introduced himself to me and immediately went on to explain that his large and very handsome black Labrador dog was running rings around him. He continued by telling me that he had beaten the dog until his hands were sore, and kicked him until he had actually hurt his foot. Needless to say, the dog was beyond help because he assumed that all forms of chastisement for all crimes were the same – a roaring voice and a beating. The dog had become immune to punishment.

There is also the example of another Labrador who was brought to my kennels for training. He arrived, sitting comfortably on the lap of the owner's wife, who could barely be seen as she peered out from behind this large dog she was cradling like a child. I had him in my kennel for a few months and he was duly collected by his owner. The dog was fully trained and a good working dog. His abilities were demonstrated and off he went, his owner highly satisfied. A few weeks later, however, the owner was on the telephone, full of tales of woe about his dog running in and generally running wild.

I asked him to bring the dog back so I could see for myself the amazing regression in a dog that had only recently left my hands well trained. True enough, when we went out into the field the dog paid no attention to his owner as he ran this way and that. He shot a dummy for the dog (using my dummy launcher) and the dog was after it in a flash, ignoring his shouting and blowing of the whistle. I had been watching this scene unfold, trying not to let the dog see me. Eventually I called the dog over to me. I gave him a clip round the ear, told him to walk to heel, and off we set.

As if by magic the dog behaved himself impeccably, sitting when I stopped and, when I shot a dummy, sitting patiently while I collected it. Then I shot another, which the dog retrieved beautifully to hand on command. The owner was astonished. What, he enquired, was the reason for such different behaviour? I told him quite honestly that the dog had realized he was a mug. Knowing he would get away with it, he had been allowed to do as he pleased – and was happy to do so. I gave the owner a lesson how – and when – to administer discipline, pointing out to him that, unless he wanted the dog to completely take over and make a fool him, he had no alternative. He telephoned me a few weeks later to report that the dog was doing extremely well, and the problems had disappeared. A perfect example of a man whose attitude was too soft.

Another good example is a beautiful Flat-coated Retriever bitch who came in for training. She walked to heel well, pacing herself to the speed I walked at during training sessions, was well mannered and sat immediately I stopped. Yet when the same dog went out for a walk with her owner – a young woman who lived nearby – she immediately began to play up. The dog's experience with her owner was of playful indulgence and when walking to heel on the lead she continually walked with her head and neck bent in front of the owner's legs, looking up at her, causing her to either bump into the dog or trip and stumble. Rather than forcibly jerking the dog back into the heel position, she was more likely to give her an apologetic tug, which was a momentary inconvenience to the dog. When this dog sat at my feet when I stopped, she sat to one side as she had been trained to do, and patiently looked about her. When the owner asked the dog to do the same thing, she would not sit patiently and continually jumped to her feet, wagging her tail and wanting to play.

It is often said that there is no such thing as a bad dog, only bad owners, and there is certainly a great deal of truth in that. Irrespective of how well trained a young dog is it is the owner's attitude that governs the dog's behaviour. So it is absolutely imperative, whenever you are training a dog, to fully realize the importance of achieving a balance of respect and affection, and not to have a soft attitude, crediting the dog with human emotions or intelligence. Remember that a dog will take its lead from the attitude of its owner, and consistency is vital at all times.

* * * * * *

Before moving on to the next stage in the training of your dog it is worthwhile reiterating that you are not in a race, so have patience with your dog; time is very much on your side. If your dog is nine months old now but you are nowhere near the levels suggested in this chapter, do not rush him along in order to catch up. By the same token do not take things so slowly that your young dog is fast losing interest in the whole affair. If you are having problems with any aspect of the training to date, stand back, and look at the problem with an objective eye, go back to square one and work the problem through. Your intelligence is far greater than the dog's so use it, outsmart him when you feel it necessary, and trick him into resolving the problems. Don't skim over the surface and assume that these troubles will go away as the dog gets older. They won't. You and your dog together must resolve the problems. Use your common sense now and always when training your dog, and you should find that things will go smoothly.

## Summary

In this chapter we have introduced the young dog to tasks and commands he will need to learn if he is to be the gundog you desire. What we have covered in the last three months:

- Walking to heel on and off the lead.
- Sitting (and staying) on 'sit', to hand signal and to whistle.
- Coming to you on voice, to hand signal and to whistle.
- Early retrieving – but only one in six (remember to use the wind).
- Introduction to water.
- Don't forget the basic discipline and remember not to shout.
- When to punish and when to reward.

# 6

# BECOMING AN ADOLESCENT

Before every new phase of training, it is a good idea to appraise the progress of your young dog by setting aside the occasional day when you run through all the training that has been achieved to date, rather than doing practise and training on the same day.

Go to your normal training ground and run through everything you have done with your dog so far, giving him a minimum of commands, and those that you do, give quietly and directly. Walk him to heel on the lead. When you stop he should sit. At the pat of a thigh and the command, 'walk on' he should walk on with you. With the lead removed he should walk to heel, sitting when you stop, and should remain where you have left him on the additional command of 'sit', allowing you to walk on as far as you wish, before you turn and walk back to him. Collecting him, he should again walk well to heel. He should sit on command to voice, whistle or hand, whether he is running towards you or going away, and allow you to throw dummies all around him, which you then pick up. He should also retrieve whichever dummy you tell him to fetch, bringing it nicely to hand. He should enjoy entering water.

This early part of your dog's training is the foundation stone on which you will build all his training. Without good, solid, confident obedience at this stage, it is pointless continuing. You can polish and hone your dog's abilities over the next year or so until he is absolutely superb – but only if these early training routines are firmly imbedded in the dog's head and his reactions are crisp and perfect. Any deviation or slackness at this stage in not acceptable and must be perfected before you move on, since if a dog does not have a firm grasp of everything that is expected of him so far, then the rest of his training will be built on shaky ground. Everything else you are going to train the dog to do are refinements and extensions of this early training.

## The feathered dummy

Up until now your dog will have retrieved only canvas covered dummies. Now you are about to add a new and more exciting dimension, that of the feathered dummy and, if done correctly, this normally goes off without any problems. But – as with all other aspects of training your dog – when you introduce him to a new experience you must assume that things will not go perfectly and never take anything for granted.

The best type of feathered dummy is made up of a light canvas dummy, with two closed pheasant's wings firmly bound on either side. Take your dog to your normal training area, throw one normal dummy and send the dog on a retrieve. He will, as he has been used to doing, dash out, grab the dummy and bring it to hand. Leave him in a sitting position, immediately throw the feathered dummy into the wind and send him for it with the 'fetch' command. As he nears it, encourage him on with it, calling 'steady' and when he picks the dummy, shout 'good boy, good boy', 'good girl, good girl', or similar encouraging noises. Often, if approached in this way, you will discover that he rushes out and grabs the dummy, completely unaware of either its different texture or consistency and will run back to you. If this is the case, then his introduction to the feathered dummy will have been effected without fuss and from now on, all dummies used should be feathered ones.

However, it is possible that when the dog reaches the dummy he will either be immediately aware that the smell is different, or that the feel in his mouth is different. It is unlikely that any dog which is used to picking up a canvas dummy would refuse to pick it up – particularly if, as he is approaching it, you give him encouragement. If he does refuse to pick it, put it away and don't try him on a feathered dummy for another week. Then try him on the feathered dummy at weekly intervals until he eventually picks it up.

A more likely problem is that of the dog running back towards you with the feathered dummy, shaking it vigorously, or appearing reluctant to bring it straight to you. If there is any reluctance, immediately squat down, calling him on, or alternatively, run backwards from him and when he does bring the retrieve to you give him much praise.

If he grabs the dummy and starts to shake it, employ exactly the same tactics by encouraging him on, getting him to run after you, and take the dummy from him as soon as you can. Problems with the introduction of the feathered dummy normally resolve themselves by a combination of familiarity of this new type of dummy, and the simple expedient of taking a week before asking the dog to pick up the feathered dummy again. However, in my experience, any problems encountered at this stage are purely temporary, and with a little patience will go away. Whatever you do, no matter how frustrating you feel the situation is – particularly if the dog seems reluctant to return to you with the dummy – do not chase him and do not chastize him. Gently encourage him, and when he does bring the dummy to you, make a fuss of him.

After your dog is converted to retrieving the feathered dummy, introduce him to the fur dummy, which is simply made by taking a piece of dried rabbit skin and binding it firmly around your canvas dummy. Then using exactly the same technique as with the feathered dummy, throw the (by now familiar) feathered dummy for a first retrieve, immediately followed by the fur one. The technique for solving any problems that may crop up is exactly the same as before.

Once you have your dog retrieving the fur or feathered dummy, keep ringing the changes. Whilst it is never a good idea to give a dog too many retrieves in any one training session, you can, by now, get him up to two retrieves per training period – with three occasionally – always endeavouring to mix the texture of the retrieves you want him to pick.

Remember, in all retrieving exercises the golden rule is that for every retrieve you throw for your dog, you must have thrown three which you have retrieved yourself while he sits watching you. You must avoid at all costs any dog getting it into his head that a retrieve is automatically his property, otherwise you are encouraging the crime of running in, chasing game, and generally being unsteady. Throughout his life he must always regard any retrieve on which he is sent as a privilege, as a reward, but never as either his right or that the retrieve is his property.

*Throwing dummies to either side for more advanced retrieving training. Leaving your arm outstretched until the dummy lands helps build the foundation of hand signals.* (JAMES DOUGLAS)

# The sound of shooting – an introduction

It is quite surprising how many people think that the idea of introducing a dog to shot is simply a matter of taking a very small puppy, firing a gun directly over its head, and finding out if he is afraid! Such techniques are not only extremely foolish but can cause problems that did not exist until such an action put them there. The sudden and unexpected loud bang from a shotgun, fired at close range over a young dog that has never heard such a sound before, can virtually frighten it out of its wits, make it flinch, and cause it to view a gun as an instrument of fright every time it appears. Therefore the introduction to shot should always follow exactly the same routine.

Enlist the aid of a friend, and get him or her to walk 100 metres or so away. Sit beside your dog, talking to it and comforting it. On a pre-arranged signal from you your assistant should fire a shot in the air using a starting pistol. Watch your dog and give him encouragement. The dog will obviously react to the shot, in that he will turn his head and look in the direction from where it came. Have your friend fire another shot, while you make a fuss of your dog. Then progressively, your assistant should come twenty paces closer before firing another shot at your hand signal. Continue in this way. Watch your dog carefully. If he shows any sign of fear, stop the lesson immediately and start again a few days later.

Dogs fall into three distinct categories when it comes to a shot being fired:

- Those to whom it means absolutely nothing and who will eventually learn to regard the shot as heralding a likely retrieve.
- Those that are gun nervous and are disconcerted at the bang and will require a much longer introductory period to instil the confidence in them that there is nothing to be alarmed about.
- Those who are gun shy, which is a major problem that cannot be solved.

Gun shyness is an inherited trait that should not be confused with the caution and trepidation of a dog that is gun nervous. A gun shy dog will just simply never come to terms with the noise of a gun and will, in fact, quickly get to recognize the gun as the creator of this terrible noise, and many will run at the sight of the gun without a shot being fired. A gun shy dog will either cower timidly against your legs at the sound of a shot, or more normally will run away, either standing a long distance off from you, quaking in fear or will often take to his heels and, ignoring your calls, either run all the way to your car, or back home.

It makes no sense whatsoever to keep a gun shy dog. It will never make a gundog, and the best advice for anyone is to advertize the dog as a pet, and either do not pass on the pedigree or write in ink across the corner of it the reason for the dog being sold, in an attempt to prevent any unscrupulous individual breeding with the dog and perpetuating the problem. Personally I would have the dog either spayed or castrated, then I know it is impossible.

A good guide to how much to charge when selling a dog which is not making the grade as a gundog, but is otherwise a good dog, is to ask the current price of a new puppy, plus the cost of its inoculations. In this way a fair price is struck, giving the new owner a dog at a good price, which will have had quite a bit of its discipline training already completed, and therefore make it more desirable as a pet. At the same time this makes the pill that bit easier for you to swallow, since at least you have recouped the basic costs of starting again.

*Introducing the dog to the sound of shots. Note the starting pistol behind the trainer's back.*
(JAMES DOUGLAS)

Gun shyness and gun nervousness should not be confused. A dog which is gun nervous should get over it. In fact, one of my own best bitches, when first introduced to shot was distinctly unhappy about the whole experience. So if your dog appears to be alarmed, frightened, or cautious at the appearance of your starting pistol or gun, do not assume that it is gun shy. Rather apply a bit of intelligence and patience before deciding that it is beyond hope.

## The dummy launcher

As soon as your young dog is happy at the sound of your starting pistol, it is time to introduce the use of the dummy launcher. The best method of effecting the introduction of this is to sit the dog at a distance – say twenty metres away from you. Let him see the starting pistol and fire it. The sight of it and the familiar shot will prepare him for the slightly sharper bang of the launcher, plus the new sensation of a simultaneous obstacle flying through the air. Keeping the dog at twenty metres from you, produce the dummy launcher. Push the dummy not more than half way down the spigot, load it and fire it at a slight angle above the parallel to the ground, and shoot it at a right angle to you and the dog. In this way he can see both you and the launcher being fired, and will pick up the missile as it flies away.

By putting it half way down the spigot you effectively reduce the power of the firing blank and the dummy will only go a short distance – approximately twenty-five metres – the distance of a hand-thrown dummy. Do not be tempted to push the dummy all the way down the spigot at this stage, or you will launch the dummy much further (approximately eighty metres) than the dog has been used to working from you.

Watch the dog's reaction. It should be no more than one of slight surprise. Then retrieve the dummy yourself. Repeat the process. Retrieve it yourself again, then shoot it a third time, and this time, after the dummy has landed, wave the dog after the retrieve with the command to 'fetch' and give him the line to follow, with your arm pointing towards the dummy. In this introduction to the dummy launcher always make sure – where possible – to throw the first few retrieves into short grass where the dog can see the retrieve. Take it from the dog, give him praise and put the dummy launcher away. The lesson is finished for the day. When training a dog it is always better to finish on a high note.

Thereafter continue to use the dummy launcher in subsequent training periods, gradually allowing the dog to come closer when you shoot, until eventually you are shooting the dummy launcher when he is sitting beside you. Remember always to command him to sit, in preparation for the dropping to shot lesson he will be taught fairly soon.

Progressively, over the next few weeks, push the dummy further down the spigot until the dog is being sent the full eighty to one hundred metres. The distance you send your young dog on retrieves obviously depends on the sort of ground you are training him on. A young dog that is used to being sent on retrieves some twenty-five metres away, is going to have to be gradually worked out further. There is no point in expecting an inexperienced young dog – irrespective of how good he seems to be at marking the line of a fallen dummy – to dash eighty metres through long bracken. That would be most unwise, and in the initial stages of the use of the dummy launcher restrict the long retrieves at a maximum shot range, to short grass, where the dog is given the visual aid of seeing the dummy fall. At the same time you can keep the dog in sight at all times, so you can correct or aid him if he starts to lose the place.

## From a distance

One of the most necessary controls you must have over any gundog is to be able to stop the dog at distance quickly and efficiently. There really is no reason why a dog should sit perfectly well on command ten metres from you and not drop with equally crisp efficiency 125 metres away. Yet distance control is one of those thorny areas where many people find problems. The reasons for these problems are either a sloppiness in the training at close hand – with the owner neither expecting nor getting crisp obedience – or the dog has discovered what I call 'the influence barrier'. This is the magical distance the dog has discovered when he knows that once he has passed it he is out of your control.

How often have you heard people say that their dog is perfect close at hand, but once it reaches a distance away – normally about fifty metres – he ignores them? The reason is usually that the dog has misbehaved – perhaps spent time sniffing a tasty scent at a distance – and the owner has accepted this delay or lack of attention, rather than getting after the dog immediately, bring him to heel and enforcing his will.

The other reason that people have difficulty at distance is because of the dog's lack of confidence when he is far away from you. The dog feels insecure and remote from the handler. All the problems can be avoided if the owner has diligently stuck to the correct training schedule when the dog was younger. If the dog has been told to sit and remain while you walk long distances away before returning; if he has been taught to sit to the whistle when coming towards you, then he will sit automatically when the whistle sounds. With a little practice, the sound of the whistle, heard at distance (and therefore quieter) will mean the same as the loud whistle heard close at hand.

By now your dog will be sitting with hand, whistle and voice commands, and his reaction to any of these commands should be automatic. Whistle control at a distance is really just a case of stretching the distance between you and your dog, always striving to put greater distances between you.

Start off with the now familiar routine of leaving him sitting and walking a long distance away. Go out of sight and hide behind a tree or wall, or any hiding place where he cannot see you, but you can peer round. Keep your eye on him. At the first sign of him standing up, or curiosity, reappear and firmly blow the whistle and command him to sit. Hopefully he will not be tempted to jump to his feet, but if he does you must realize that he is only anxious that you have gone off and left him. The object of this exercise is to enforce on the dog the ability to remain where he is left until you return and collect him. At the same time you will be building in his mind a growing confidence in sitting alone, without you there as reassurance. This confidence building is vitally important, and, when you reappear after a few minutes you must always remember to return to the dog nine times out of ten, letting him come to you only once. This will instil in his mind the confidence that you will always return.

You can call him to you occasionally at distance with the recall signal (several small toots) just to keep him sharp. Do not, however, be tempted to call him to you too often, otherwise you will quickly build in his mind the anticipation that he is about to be called to you and you will soon discover his hindquarters off the ground ready to spring after you, rather than the desired relaxed feeling of him sitting in the confident knowledge that there is no need to worry since you are sure to return.

The essence of distance control is, as I have said previously, continually stretching the distance between you and the dog as you give him a command. He will by now sit confidently fifty metres from you, come on the recall, and drop at the sound of your whistle, when he is twenty-five metres from you. With care and systematic stretching of distance you will soon find that you can blow the whistle commanding him to stop if you leave him at 100 metres, calling him in and stopping at, say, fifty metres.

There is, however, one danger area in the recall command, and it is one which you must watch for signs of in the dog. And that is the dog beginning to anticipate the sit command as he is running towards you. Having left your dog, let us say 100 metres away, and having got him used to being called – then dropped half way – watch for hesitancy in the dog when he runs towards you. Is he running at a slower speed, as though waiting for the command to sit as you blow your whistle? If you see your dog behaving like this, give him a period when you call him to you and do not command him to sit half way, before returning to the lesson. Always remember that in all dog training it is essential to ring the changes. Never do the same thing too often in succession, or you will encourage your dog to anticipate commands, which is undesirable.

## Hand signals at a distance

It is at distance that the sense of using the obvious and exaggerated hand signals will become apparent. A dog watching you from about 50 to 150 metres can clearly see your silhouette. An arm held in front of you is lost in the silhouette, whereas an arm stuck straight in the air can be seen clearly. Equally, thigh patting – to bring your dog to you – should be a big movement. Your straightened arm should come up at right angles to your body at shoulder height, and move up and down from the thigh.

One problem that many people encounter is when they leave their young dog in a sitting position and walk away from him. They throw the dummy and stand for a few moments before directing the dog. The instant they utter a sound or make a movement the dog anticipates the command and is away on the retrieve.

The way to avoid this is simple. Keeping your eye on the dog make a sound – any sound – and move your arms. If the dog makes any attempt to move, immediately command him to sit. The idea is for you to be able to stand in front of your dog at any distance, to jump up and down and sing at the top of your voice while your dog sits motionless, watching you. Only when you give him a specific hand signal does he spring into action.

## Retrieving from water

Whilst most of your retrieving work will have been done on land, you should have been building in a proportion of water retrieves and teaching competence in water. Often this depends on the proximity of water to your training areas, some trainers being forced to make a specific trip when water is not close. Wherever possible you should have given the dog retrieves of the hand-thrown dummy either from water or across water. The idea is simply to use the water as another location from which the dog must retrieve. After your dog has been introduced to the dummy launcher, and is coming along with his land retrieves, you can start to incorporate the launcher into his normal water work. Be careful not to ask the dog to swim too far at this stage, since it is

*Young Springer Spaniel showing lots of confidence with this water retrieve.* (JAMES DOUGLAS)

inappropriate to send a young dog on a long swim out and back. The distance you ask him to swim should be carefully increased in direct proportion to his growing confidence and stamina. The real benefit of the dummy launcher with water work comes from the combination of the shot, which makes him sit as he looks about expectantly, and the dummy flying much further than you can throw it, and encouraging him to mark.

Care should be taken with water retrieves, since this is the one element where you cannot pick the retrieve yourself. So give him a restricted number of water retrieves in any training period – no more than one or two – and try always to follow water retrieving by making the dog sit while you pick two or three retrieves yourself from land.

## The shot as a signal to drop

After your dog has become quite happy and relaxed at the sound of your starting pistol, and has been introduced to the dummy launcher, when he will have been taught to sit prior to it being used, you can start to teach him to drop to shot. This is a comparatively easy lesson to teach.

Sit the dog fifty metres from you, call him in to you, and when he is perhaps twenty-five metres away, throw your arm in the air – as for the visual command to sit – and at the same time blow the whistle command to sit, or give the verbal command. Have the starting pistol in your left hand behind your back and, as you command him to sit, fire the pistol. He should automatically sit to the familiar commands (whistle and arm) although he will almost certainly look around in surprise at the unexpected bang. Keep him in the sitting position for a few minutes before repeating the exercise. He will have sat to the familiar whistle, hand or voice command, and will soon associate the pistol shot with sitting – and you will have taught him to drop to shot.

More important is the time when you move to doing this exercise with the dog facing away from you. Cast him out and when he has his back to you blow the stop command on the whistle, at the same time firing a shot. If you have done the correct amount of groundwork with your whistle he should sit immediately. After a few lessons you should be able to stop the use of the other aids and use the pistol shot only as a command to sit.

## Walls, fences and other obstacles

The ability to cross obstacles, and the self-confidence to tackle walls, streams and fences, must be encouraged and brought out in all dogs. They have a natural ability to jump, but this ability can be refined and developed so that you instil in your dog confidence to launch himself at obstacles which would be daunting for an untrained dog. Personally, I am not happy with a dog that does not jump on command, but I would never put a dog over a strand fence. I have seen them not only break their leg, but also injure themselves by jumping barbed wire fences. I always teach a dog to go through such a fence when I open the wires.

### Strand fences
Sit your dog at your feet beside the fence. Open the fence, parting the wires with your left hand and foot, and throw a dummy through, encouraging the dog to go through after it. If necessary, you can gently push the dog through the fence, giving him encouragement at the same time. Most dogs quickly learn this and it should be practised regularly in the training routine.

*Encouraging a young Labrador to overcome obstacles, in this case by squeezing through between the wires. Note the young Spaniel patiently waiting for its turn.* (JAMES DOUGLAS)

*A young Springer Spaniel looking very confident as it learns to jump fences.* (JAMES DOUGLAS)

Low tightly-strung sheep or rabbit fencing where there is little chance of the dog getting caught in the fence is the best place to teach a dog to jump. Cross the fence and walk on, encouraging the dog to follow you. He will either jump the fence and follow you (and thereafter require only practice) or, more likely, he will run up and down the fence in confusion.

Return to the fence, bring him to heel, let him know you are happy with him, produce the dummy and throw it over the fence where he can see it. Then lift him and drop him over the other side, Once a dog has been shown a couple of times what is expected, I have never known them not to take to this exercise. Remember that the command to cross a fence is 'over' and at all times from now on, whenever you put your dog over a fence, command it clearly with the simple word 'over'.

## Walls

Since they have footholds and are not as confusing to the dog as a fence, which he can see through, walls are easier for him to jump. Therefore, a dummy thrown over a wall would normally encourage the dog to find its own way over. If your dog is reluctant to jump the wall, another technique is for you to sit on top of the wall and encourage him to follow you. He should normally then stand up against the wall, anxiously trying to get after you. All you do then is haul him up and let him drop over the other side or else simply cross the wall and call him over.

When you first introduce your dog to a wall as an obstacle over which he must cross, it is obviously desirable to start with a low wall, throwing the dummy over and commanding him to retrieve it, saying the word 'over' as he approaches the wall. Then it should be a simple matter of progressing to higher walls which the dog must climb over.

## Streams

Crossing a narrow stream can be strangely confusing for some young dogs. You cross it in one stride and yet many young dogs will run up and down the bank in confusion before – apparently in desperation – launching themselves across. Encourage your dog over, as before, and all should be well.

Once a young dog has learned to jump, it is a comparatively easy task to systematically increase the distance that you expect him to jump. There is obviously a limitation as to how high a dog can jump over a fence with comfort and safety. Yet I have seen a small Labrador run straight towards a two metre high rough stone wall, launch himself up the wall, take a foothold and pull himself over. Even more surprising, I have seen him doing this carrying a goose in his mouth, and this only a few short months after he was introduced to the fact that he could jump at all. It boils down to building self-confidence in the dog.

# Quartering for spaniels and pointers

All the other chapters in this book relate to the training of all gundogs. The only area where spaniels and pointers differ from retrievers is that spaniels are required to hunt, quarter and drop to flush, and pointers are required to hunt, quarter, point and drop to flush. A retriever is used to hunt for dead or wounded game and the handler usually has a good idea of where the dog needs to concentrate its search as well as how many birds the dog should find. Hunting for live game is a much less certain activity. Neither you nor your dog knows what game is on the beat – if any – nor exactly where it will be found.

It is on the rough shoot, the grouse moors or in the beating line that we ask our dogs to hunt for live game, either to flush it so that a walking gun can shoot it as it gets up, or to drive it over a line of standing guns. Where we are hoping to shoot game over our dogs it is obviously vital that when the bird or rabbit is flushed that it is within range of the guns and for this reason a spaniel must work within a few metres of its handler. Pointing dogs, whether they are HPRs, pointers or setters, can roam out a lot farther because, once they have located game they point, rather than flushing and should hold their point for as long as it takes for the guns to come up to them. In either case though, the foundation on which quality hunting is built is good, methodical quartering.

The art of quartering is purely a refined extension of your dog's natural abilities. It is you who shapes a nice uniform pattern for your dog, as he covers the ground in front of you, searching for any game that may be hidden and either flushing or pointing the game. A spaniel, working within a few metres of the gun, will probably find any game on his beat even if his quartering pattern is less than ideal, but for a pointer, particularly when working on a grouse moor or hunting partridges through autumn stubble fields, proper quartering is absolutely essential to avoid missing birds.

How fast should your dog work? The eventual aim in any quartering dog is that it should cover its ground efficiently, miss nothing, and move at a speed which allows you to walk comfortably at your normal shooting pace. I am a great believer in the guide to game finding, given by a Seminole American Indian to Howard Hill, the American bowhunter: 'walk little, look much'. Exactly the same motto applies to the modern rough shooter. You do not want a dog that covers ground like some canine missile, compelling you to bound along just to keep up or continually have to check the dog. To enjoy shooting correctly you must walk slowly, which not only gives you time to take any shot that may arise, but allows you to take your time and enjoy the sport. So you must try to set a pattern in your dog, so that he works at the sort of speed you want to walk – neither too fast nor too slow. Conversely, a dog which potters, trundling from one scent to another is every bit as undesirable as the opposite and speedy extreme.

The only difference between a spaniel quartering and the work of an HPR, a pointer or a setter is the range which the dog works. The spaniel should always work within shotgun range. I believe a spaniel should not quarter any further than ten to fifteen metres on either side of the gun, whereas an HPR should ideally work about thirty to forty metres on either side of the gun on low ground where the cover is thick. On the open hill pointers and setters and HPRs routinely work as much as 200 metres out from the guns, depending on the ground and the numbers of grouse. Working on partridges in stubble fields in the autumn also requires pointing dogs to work well away from their handlers. Unless they are working on exceptionally wide open areas it would be normal for a pointing dog to range the full width of any field less than perhaps 200 metres across. If the field is much wider than that it could be worked in two beats, though there are pointers that will happily range over quite astounding distances without missing a bird and, where game is scarce, the more ground the dog can cover the better your chance of a shot.

Such distances may be routine for the experienced working pointer, but when you are starting out to introduce a young dog to quartering a much more restricted pattern is in order. In the early days it is much better for a dog to stay too close than for it to range too widely. There will be plenty of opportunity for him to get out and cover great distances after he has mastered the art of quartering under your control.

There are two techniques used for teaching quartering. One involves the use of assistants, which I do not recommend since I believe the dog tends to divide his attention between the handler and the assistants. However, it is worthwhile mentioning here if you feel you would be happier working in this way and can persuade two helpers to spend enough of their free time assisting you.

Having first walked all game out of a large field, the handler takes his dog to the side of the field where he is downwind. Then he sets off walking into the wind and casts the dog forward with a wave of his arm and the command 'get on'. The two assistants, who are walking directly parallel to the handler but about twenty metres distance on either side of him, start to alternate in calling the dog, as all three of them walk forward slowly. In this fashion, they all walk across the field with the dog running first this way and then that in front of the handler, who waves the dog on in the direction it is being called as it passes him. Whilst this technique works, I find it clumsy and much prefer to train dogs to quarter with the handler alone.

*With whistle at the ready, demonstrating the exaggerated arm movement used when teaching a young Spaniel to quarter.* (JAMES DOUGLAS)

*Use of the check cord to teach steadiness to this young Pointer working on a grouse moor.* (DAVID HUDSON)

The handler should walk in a zigzag course. As he starts to walk forward he gives the command 'get on' with a large and obvious wave of the arm. The dog will naturally run forward in front of the handler. When he reaches ten metres for spaniels and thirty metres for pointers, the handler gives two or three peeps on the whistle – the recall signal – and immediately turns in the other direction. The dog will race after the handler, and as he passes the handler will give him the command to 'get on' with a big wave of the arm. The dog will naturally run forward, whereupon the handler, when the dog reaches ten metres for spaniels and thirty metres for pointers on this side, gives the recall signal again, and turns away.

The dog quickly learns to enjoy this exercise because he is being allowed to move unrestricted over the ground doing what his own instincts urge him to do – to run on testing the scents. As the dog becomes more proficient at running to one side and the other, the handler can progressively make the actual distance he walks in a zigzag less before turning, until eventually the dog is running from side to side, with only the aid of the whistle to turn him and the arm wave to send him on.

The excitement of running free and hunting can quickly go to the head of some dogs with the result that the turn whistle is ignored, particularly in the case of pointers and HPRs that are working well away from their handler. A check cord – a length of light but strong line attached to the dog's collar – can be invaluable in ensuring that the dog stays under the control of the handler. The check cord can only be used where there is little or no vegetation otherwise it will quickly get tangled around every bush and shrub on the beat. It therefore is of limited use to the spaniel trainer, but it can be a vital part of the armoury for the trainer of HPRs and pointers where the distance between handler and dog is much greater and the ground hunted is often reasonably open.

If the end of the cord is left loose, without a handle to get snagged among the grass or heather, the dog will hardly feel any drag from the line as it runs. If your dog is too enthusiastic in his running you can tie a short length of stick to the loose end and let him drag it, though you should only do this in open fields where there is no danger of the stick getting caught in the undergrowth. Any object tied to the line imposes a considerable drag on the dog and you can easily confirm this for yourself by walking a few yards with a loose line in your hand, then repeating the experiment with a stick attached. While some form of drag on the end of the line can be useful for curbing an excessively enthusiastic dog there are some dogs that simply won't run with the constant tug of a line against their collars.

A thin line is best for use as a check cord, but it is essential that you wear gloves when using it. It is all too easy to end up with very painful rope burns on your hands if you try to grab the line when there is a dog at full gallop on the other end. Initially you can keep hold of the end of the line, peeping on the whistle to turn the dog just before it goes taut. Once he is responding well to this you can let the line go so that it drags freely behind the dog. If he starts pulling out too far, or ignoring his turn whistle, wait until he crosses in front of you again and catch up the line. Then, as he reaches the limit of his line you can sound the turn whistle and jerk him round smartly, reinforcing the lesson that he must listen and obey orders even when he is well away from you and enjoying himself galloping free.

The distance that the dog goes forward at either end of the beat will depend to a very large extent on the scenting conditions. A spaniel, hunting ten to fifteen metres away from you on either hand need only advance three or four metres on each cast, but if you are on the open hill with a pointer going twice the length of a football pitch on every cast you would only advance very, very slowly if he took in the same amount of ground as the spaniel. If scent is good it is not unusual for a pointer to go forward as much as fifty metres on each cast, and still find every bird on the beat. Naturally, there are days when the scent is more difficult, but on those days the experienced dog will restrict his own pattern to match the conditions.

The young dog, learning his trade in a field that is bare of game, has neither the experience nor the scent of birds to guide him. Some dogs will exhibit a tendency to try and take in great bites of ground on every cast, boring into the wind for half the length of the field before turning back across the wind. If this is the case use your turn whistle to bring the dog round within what seems like a reasonable distance from your point of view, but beware of being too restrictive. A 'shoe-polisher' – a dog that only takes in a minimum of ground on every cast – may look very neat and efficient in his work, and he certainly shouldn't miss much game, but he is actually working very inefficiently and wasting a great deal of energy in racing unnecessarily backwards and forwards while covering much of the same ground on each cast.

The quartering technique soon becomes imbedded into the dog's mind as a pattern, and after considerable practice he will naturally pace himself and turn before the handler has peeped the whistle. Work diligently with your dog at quartering until you achieve a really nice efficient technique. One method of achieving this is to walk at right angles across the line of a ploughed field, casting your dog from one side to the other. Most dogs will tend to quarter to each side of you, using the line of the furrows as a guide, and it certainly is a great aid in tidying up the crispness of the line a dog will quarter on. Of course, you should ensure that the breeze is blowing at right angles to the furrows before trying this, so that the dog is not encouraged to ignore the wind while hunting.

A problem many inexperienced handlers find when teaching quartering is that the dog will not go out far enough. Don't be concerned however. When learning to quarter it is better for a young dog to do shorter quartering which is controlled, rather than longer distance quartering, since once he gets into the field with wild game and he experiences actual shooting days, he will naturally pull out anyway.

As a good example, I have seen a pointer which quartered twenty-five metres on either side of the handler and seemed reluctant to stretch the range, to the point where the handler became quite frustrated. He asked me how he should go about getting further distance. I advised him to do nothing, since it was preferable that the dog quartered as beautifully as he did at that time in his development. Over a subsequent shooting season the dog learned, when out working in a stubble field, to draw that bit further out, turning on the whistle. He needed only two reminders of where to turn before setting himself into the pattern of quartering that particular field. The same dog, when working a grouse moor, will pull out even further. Therefore, if you have a dog who has a tendency to turn shorter than you would ideally want, it is not normally a problem, since once they gain experience in the field they will naturally pull out that bit further.

Once your dog is quartering nicely you must start judiciously dropping him on occasions, increasing your control of him. Watch until he is at full gallop, then blow the stop whistle and make sure that he responds immediately. A dangerous area of behaviour – often overlooked until it is too late – is one of the quartering dog becoming so hyped-up on the quartering exercise that he forgets he is working with you. However do not overdo the exercise of stopping him when quartering too often otherwise you may make him hesitant. It is desirable only to achieve a balance of control, rather than have the dog constantly expecting your command to drop.

Once again, the check cord can be useful in overcoming any problems that arise when getting the dog drop to command when he is running at full gallop. A signal from the drop whistle reinforced by a sharp tug on the line is a handy reminder if there are signs that his discipline is becoming slack, and it lets him know that you are still in charge and can enforce your commands even when he is some distance away from you.

Obviously, the speed at which a dog will quarter in short grass is different from that which is required in cover, but your control of the dog and his understanding of turning to the whistle – which keeps that invisible communication line between the two of you – must be absolutely unbroken before you move on to working him in more difficult sort of terrain.

When you first move to quartering him in cover it is best to keep in either long grass, a root field, or any form of vegetation where he will be slowed down and where he cannot see more than a few feet ahead. It is essential when first moving a young dog into cover that you don't lose sight of him. Only after he has progressed to quartering in short cover and responding to the whistle

*Quietly approaching a Pointer as it stands staunchly on point on a covey of grouse.* (DAVID HUDSON)

should you move to longer cover such as bracken, brambles or similar thickets. It is vital you remember that he must be utterly reliable before you move him to the sort of situation where he is out of your sight. Otherwise you will not be able to see misdemeanours as they take place and take appropriate action.

A typical problem that the handler can face when he puts the dog to cover prematurely is that of the dog coming across a rabbit and, rather than dropping to flush or coming on point, he takes a few hesitant steps after the fleeing animal. Because he is out of your sight and you are unable to stop him, this is the moment when he first realizes that perhaps he can chase undetected. I have, on more than one occasion, seen the results of premature introduction to cover, and once the bad habit is started, it can be the very devil to stop. So it is much better to be on the safe side and avoid the temptation for a young dog until the lesson is thoroughly learnt.

You should always be conscious of the direction of the wind during these early quartering lessons and try to ensure that you work straight into the wind so that the dog is quartering across the wind and turning into it at either end of the beat. Gundogs find game almost entirely by scenting it and they can only do this when the breeze is drifting the scent from the bird or rabbit down to the dog. Spaniels, and to a lesser extent, HPRs also hunt out their quarry using ground scent, getting their noses down on a line and tracking the game, but pointers and setters work on air scent – the smell of the bird carried directly from its body to the dog. Running across the wind maximizes their chances of finding game and the easiest way of doing this is to work them into the wind.

As they become more experienced they must also learn to work across the wind and even with the wind directly behind them and we will look more closely at this in the section on pointing.

*Gently encouraging the Pointer to rode in and flush a covey of grouse.* (DAVID HUDSON)

*Whistle ready and hand raised to steady this Gordon Setter as the covey it was pointing takes wing.* (DAVID HUDSON)

## Pointing (for HPRs, pointers and setters)

Some pointers will start to point from an early age. I have a young pointer puppy in my home who diligently points my wife's cat – under chairs, tables or wherever the cat is currently trying to seek refuge – and the young dog is completely untrained. Of course, he is pointing on sight rather than scent, but it is a good illustration of just how strong the instinct to point is among the pointing breeds. Conversely, other dogs may take some time before this natural instinct starts to develop – and pointing is a natural instinct. It is you, the trainer, who enhances, sculpts, shapes and develops what is just unborn. Don't concern yourself or panic if your pointer is over a year old and has not started to point. Concentrate on the other aspects of his training, while you wait for his pointing to appear.

One method which can work, and is very popular with American trainers, is for you to take your young pointer – say four to five months old – and a long cane (one and a half metres long). Tie a bird's wing to one end of a two-metre long string which is attached to the cane by the other end. Let the dog see the wing and if he starts to point encourage him with your voice. If he tries to run after it, whip it away. Once he realizes he cannot catch the wing he should start to point.

Once you notice your dog is starting to point then it is time to give him some help. It is advisable to go about this process with careful thought. Lay out the field where you intend to work the dog, giving consideration to cover, since you want to encourage your young dog to use his nose rather than his eyes. It is therefore desirable that the dog should always find with his nose rather than see the game. Long grass is ideal. Avoid training a young pointing dog in thick cover such as bracken, where he may disappear from your sight. In all early stages of working with any young dog remember that when he is out of your sight he is able to commit small indiscretions of which you are unaware.

Having decided where you are going to work your dog then lay out either dizzied pigeons (see Chapter 8 – section entitled The rabbit pen) or birds in small cages. Then, having cleared the game off the ground, work your dog – always into the wind – towards where you know the bird is lying. When using hidden game I advise the use of a small stick marker so you know exactly where the bird is.

When the young dog comes on point, approach him slowly and cautiously, giving encouragement. Kneel beside him, gently stroking the dog and mould your hands to the dog's body. Smoothly run your hands from the head down the back and on to his flanks, and then right down to the tip of his tail. This gentle stroking is to calm and soothe the dog, keeping him in position and restraining him from any temptation to run forward. After a few minutes, without flushing the bird, gently lead the dog away. Then, when he is well away from the bird, cast him on for a fresh point on your next hidden bird.

If he is reluctant to hold his point and instead shows a tendency to creep in to the bird before you can get up to him you must find a way to steady him. In early training you will usually be quite close to the dog when he finds game, but in a shooting situation there may be quite some time between the dog pointing and the guns getting into the correct position ready for him to go in and flush the birds. A peep on the stop whistle may be all that is needed to steady him up, but if this proves inadequate you can revert to the check cord.

Now, when he points, there will be twenty or thirty metres of line trailing behind him. Get your boot on the line and you are back in control. If he starts to creep forward you can check him gently and give the command 'Steady' until he firms up on point again. Getting him to realize that he must hold his point until you order him to get on is all-important. A pointer that won't hold his points is, effectively, working as a spaniel and will have to be kept within the ten to fifteen metre range that spaniels require. If he is steady and reliable on point though he can be worked at whatever sort of distance the ground and the supply of game demands and that, after all, is the *raison d'être* of having a pointer in the first place.

It is unwise at the early stage of pointing to encourage a young dog to set up game, since all you are doing is encouraging him to run in and give chase. When you give your dog pointing experience on the captive birds, start to progressively lengthen the time you keep him on point, styling him with your hands, soothing him with your voice. An added refinement, which is not necessary but adds a bit of style, is to gently lift one of your dog's front legs whenever it is pointing feathered game, and a hind leg if it is fur.

Once you reach the stage when your young dog is coming on point and rigidly holding it, then it is time to introduce him to the command of 'put up'. With your whistle ready to make him drop, encourage the dog forward with the command 'put up'. If you are using a dizzied pigeon it may be necessary to gently slip your toe under the bird and flick it up. Immediately the bird springs, give the dog the command to sit. If the dog makes the slightest attempt to make a grab for the bird after being given the command to sit, immediately stop him with a firm 'no'. With more fiery dogs it is sometimes necessary, when working the dog in to a point, to use a long check lead so that you can gently restrain the dog from creeping forward. But try to restrict the use of the lead when flushing game to a bare minimum and dispense with it at the earliest opportunity, since a dog quickly gets to recognize the difference between the restriction of the lead and freedom.

The most undesirable fault a pointer can develop is having an unreliable point, as he gives in to the temptation of running in. Therefore a great emphasis should be made in keeping the dog rigidly on point. However, avoid allowing the dog to become so fixed in his point that he cannot be called off. Some pointers find it very difficult to break a point and only continual practice, over a period of weeks, can cure this problem, as the dog grows to learn and understand what the trainer requires of it.

Once a young pointer can point keenly and then put the game out on the command 'put up' and neatly drop to flush, the handler can use captive game less and start to work the dog on wild game. But you should not move to wild game until your dog is very confident in pointing, flushing and dropping. Pheasants in particular have a tendency to run rather than sit tightly when the dog points them and this can be a worry for the handler as the dog creeps forward to maintain contact with the running bird rather than staying solidly on point. If you insist on the dog staying still there is a danger that he will lose the bird altogether – not a desirable state of affairs in the shooting field. Conversely, having to keep creeping forward while on point may encourage the dog to become somewhat less than steady. The best solution is probably to avoid pheasants where possible when first introducing your dog to live game. Once he is more experienced he will learn to cope with running birds as well as those that sit tight.

If you already have an experienced pointer, or can enlist the aid of someone else who does, you may be able to use the older dog to find and point game and then bring your own dog in behind the point so that he can get a noseful of scent and begin to learn what it signifies. One problem that can arise when doing this is that most pointers have a tendency to 'back' another dog that is on point. Something in the sight of a dog on point triggers the pointing instinct so that the backing dog comes on to point even though he is not himself getting the scent of the game. This is a useful trait, particularly when working more than one dog because it curbs the tendency for the dogs to steal another dog's point, but it can make taking a young dog in behind another dog on point a little difficult.

While your dog has obviously been taught to quarter prior to pointing, it is at this stage that his quartering and pointing should be tightly merged into the one exercise, so that you can start to quarter him into side winds. It is ill advised to make it any more difficult for your dog than is absolutely necessary. The wise handler should always use the wind to his best advantage by working his dog into it until he reaches the standard where his dog is quartering and coming on point beautifully every time.

Don't start teaching your dog to work a side wind until he has completely mastered the technique of quartering into the wind and pointing game. It does not normally take a dog long to realize that the most efficient way of finding game is with the wind blowing straight into his face. When you get out and start shooting though it will not be possible to work into the wind at all times. Whether you are beating, rough shooting or running in a field trial, there will be times when your dog has to work with the wind coming from the side, at an angle from in front or from behind or even blowing directly from behind him. Only experience can teach him the best way of coping under all these different conditions, but you can certainly guide him in the right direction in the course of his training.

The early quartering training will have concentrated on getting the dog to work a good, even pattern while working into the wind. Once you have reached this stage with your dog you can start teaching him to work the wind, first from the side, and eventually with the wind coming from behind. Begin with a cheek wind, organizing the beat so that the wind is coming from about two o'clock on an imaginary clock face. When you cast your dog off, instead of going out at right angles to your direction of travel send him off to the left as if he was heading for ten o'clock on your imaginary dial.

When he first turns he should come back across in front of you and onwards, so that when he turns again he will actually be turning from behind your right shoulder. He should always turn into the wind at the end of each beat of course, and the effect should be that, while you are actually walking across the wind the dog is still working always at a right angle to the direction of the breeze.

The further round the wind goes the more the dog will have to work at odds with the direction in which you are walking. If the wind is directly from the side, i.e. three o' clock or nine o'clock, then the dog should be going out directly away from you and then turning to come straight back, though always working progressively across your front. In practice it is easier than it may sound, particularly since the dog, knowing how vital the scent is to his chances of finding game, will in all probability adjust his quartering pattern to suit, wherever the breeze may be coming from.

When the wind is directly at the handler's back there are two possible ways to work. In one the dog would be sent out well in front in a straight line with the 'go back' signal. He should then be stopped with the whistle and should look back at you for directions. He should then be given the visual signal of a wave to one side and the command 'get on'. If he has learned to work the wind correctly he will quarter back towards you. The distance that you send him out will depend on the ground you are working. If you were shooting over a spaniel in thick cover you would not want to send him more than perhaps thirty metres for fear that he would flush game out of range of the gun. In stark contrast, a pointing dog on a grouse moor could well go 400 or 500 metres out before quartering back.

In the shooting field this method of working a back wind can cause a few practical problems. What if your dog, having been sent 400 metres out, comes on point as soon as he starts quartering back to you? Obviously you will have to go to the point, but what if you walk up game on the way in the ground that he has not yet hunted? And when you have worked out the original point you will then have to turn back and work the dog through the ground he has missed in case there was any game that stayed hidden when you walked forward to the first point, then turn again to get back to your proper direction of travel. This can be a messy way of working a beat and cause quite a lot of unnecessary walking.

Another way of working a down wind beat is to allow the dog to quarter almost as if the wind was actually coming from in front. This will make very little difference in practice for a spaniel, working close to the handler, because any game that he flushes should still get up well within gunshot. For the HPR or pointer though there will always be the danger of birds being flushed instead of pointed because the dog, at the end of each cast will be turning down wind and can thus bump into birds before he has any chance of winding them.

When the dog comes on to point on a downwind beat the odds are that the quarry will be between the dog and the guns: in other words the dog will be pointing directly towards you instead of away from you. Some authorities recommend that, in such a case, handler and guns take a wide loop around the beat so as to come in from behind the dog, just as if he was working into the wind. In practice it is much simpler and usually a lot more effective, to walk straight towards where the dog is pointing. The odds are that the guns will walk the game up as they go in, but if the birds are sitting particularly tightly it is then a simple matter to turn when you reach the dog and allow him to go forward to hunt out the game and flush it just as he would if you were working into the wind as normal.

It should be emphasized that generally HPRs, pointers and setters get better with experience. In the use of the wind the pointer becomes more efficient as he educates his nose and learns to interpret the invisible messages he is being brought on the breeze. Knowing just how close he can get to game without flushing it prematurely, differentiating between foot scent and body scent, knowing when the scent is telling him that the birds are there, right in front of him, or that they have run, or flown in the past few minutes leaving only the traces of their scent behind can only come with experience. It can take several seasons for an HPR, pointer or setter to realize his full potential, but in many ways this only makes training and working them all the more rewarding.

## Summary

Up until this point all the work you have done with your dog has been variations on the theme of obedience, constantly emphasizing control and communication between yourself and your dog. By now he should be a well-behaved, disciplined animal. He should:

- Walk to heel and sit when you stop.
- Remain where he is until told otherwise.

- Run enthusiastically to retrieve both hand-thrown and shot dummies.
- Retrieve from water.
- Sit to the sound of shot, whistle hand and voice, either close at hand, or at distance, whether coming towards you or going away.
- Spaniels and pointers should be able to quarter in front of the gun.
- Pointers should take (and hold) a stylish and firm point.

He should generally be a pleasure to work with and his understanding of your vocabulary should have increased also. Vocal and (sometimes) visual commands learned at this stage are:

- Sit /stop
- Recall
- Walk on
- Get on
- Steady
- Fetch
- Over
- Put up (for pointers).

Whistle commands he has learned are:

- Sit /stop
- Recall.

# 7

# THE DOG'S FIRST BIRTHDAY AND BEYOND

By the time your young dog is one year old, he should be well on his way to being a gundog with a solid foundation of basic training. Over the next year you are going to train your dog in many interesting, different and highly useful actions which are all little more than variations of what you have already taught him. Because he has a good grounding in the basics it should be comparatively easy, much less frustrating and highly pleasurable for you to work with him.

Keep in mind, however, that this is not a race, and if your dog has not reached the standard that the book indicates there is no reason to be concerned. All dogs are different and, just like children, some have a capacity to learn faster and earlier than others. Some tend to be 'plodders' who develop later, and any book can only lay down guidelines of what to expect. The one thing to avoid – if you have a particularly bright dog – is not to race ahead.

It is extremely important that you are never tempted to try and advance a dog's training beyond the time guide. While your dog is still very young mentally you could take him beyond the stage of true reliability. A young dog, for instance, should not be taken shooting or introduced to dead game before his training is well advanced. If you are fortunate to have a particularly precocious one, it is more desirable to capitalize on the fact and concentrate on getting each individual lesson absolutely perfect. With all gundog training there is a simple rule: if you find your dog is having difficulty slow the training down. But if he is having no difficulty at all you can step up the training a little, but do not go too fast. Fit the schedule to the dog. It is over the next few months that you should begin to see the results of all the hard work you have done together.

## Honing up the distance work

Start off with the dog close to you; about ten metres away. Throw a hand-thrown dummy to the left, keeping him in a sitting position. If, in your preparatory work you have picked up most of the dummies yourself and always given sufficient period of time between the act of throwing the dummy and the command to retrieve it, then you should have no problems at this time. The dog should sit, watching proceedings with interest, to see whether he is going to be allowed to pick up the dummy. Giving him a big, obvious hand signal, and with the command 'fetch' wave him towards the dummy. Take the retrieve, return the dog to his former position, and repeat the exercise, this time sending the dog to the right. Over the next few sessions repeat these left and right retrieves.

Doing it this way – and taking time – normally results in the lesson being easily learnt, and after a few sessions you can progress to two dummies. You should try using a fence or wall when doing these exercises and this assists the dog to run in a straight line. If you can practise making your dog run straight – either to the right or left (and later straight away from you) – it will eventually make placing him on blind retrieves that bit easier.

With his back to a fence, stand about three metres in front of the dog and throw a dummy a short distance to the left and another to the right, against the fence. Hold your arm up in the 'sit' command and let the dog register that there are two dummies. Dogs will always naturally want to go for the last dummy thrown. This is the most immediate in the dog's mind and is obviously the one he would much prefer to pick, so – in keeping with the theory of your mind always controlling the dog's – direct him on to the first dummy thrown with the command 'fetch'. Be prepared, if he breaks toward the other dummy, to blow the stop whistle quickly and drop him, waving him back on to the one you wish him to retrieve.

If, in his excitement, the dog goes towards the second dummy and doesn't stop on the whistle, take the retrieve as though nothing had happened. When you repeat the exercise stand much closer to him so that you can physically stop him if necessary.

Return the dog to the sitting position, then wave him to retrieve the second dummy. Vary this particular exercise, increasing the distance between yourself and the dog while increasing the distance of the retrieves. It should not take too long until you have reached the stage where you can throw a dummy well to the left and right, walk a good fifty metres away from the dog and then, on the visual signal combined with the 'fetch' command, direct him to whichever dummy you want.

A variation on the direction of left and right is that of going straight away from you. This is best done – if possible – on a path. Take a dummy out, let the dog see it, then throw it a few metres back down the path you have just walked. Continue on with your dog at heel for a short distance (about ten metres), make him sit, then, standing in front of him, wave your arm straight above your head with the command 'go back'. Your dog will react in one of two ways. He will either turn and immediately run back for the dummy, or cast about unsure of what is wanted. If he casts about – obviously having forgotten about the dummy – then you have simply walked too far and let too much time pass between throwing the dummy and sending him back.

Collect the dummy yourself and repeat the exercise, this time shortening the distance you walk before sending him back. The encouraging sound of your voice as you send him is normally enough to get him dashing back for the dummy. Once he has had a few opportunities to go back he will quickly pick up this new command.

Now repeat the exercise against the fence. Sit him beside the fence, facing you. Throw the dummy over his head, walk away a few metres, then send him back, with your arm straight above your head and the command 'go back'. Practise, a little but often, is the secret. One or two retrieves during every training session should be enough. Progressively move yourself further from the dog and the retrieves further away and you will soon find that you can stand fifty metres from your dog and direct him to the left, right, or straight away from you.

## Advanced dummy retrieving – more than one at a time

When a dog has reached the level of confidence in himself and his surroundings, and is happily retrieving dummies – either thrown or shot from a launcher – you can start to move him through

*As training progresses gradually increase the distance you send him for retrieves.* (James Douglas)

a series of advanced dummy retrieving exercises. His retrieving to date will have been a mixture of dummies (fur and feather), thrown and shot, and by now he will be retrieving from water and light cover. The term 'advanced dummy retrieving' means quite literally that you can make the retrieves progressively more difficult as you strive to recreate the ever-differing retrieves and obstacles which the dog must face in his working life.

Remember that all your training is aimed at producing the sort of gundog you can be proud of; the sort of dog that you can take to a shoot, whether it is a formal driven bird or a day's rough shooting with a friend. He should be a dog that you can confidently send on any retrieve that may present itself.

You should slowly start to make the whole business of retrieving more difficult. Use your imagination to utilize whatever natural configuration the training ground has. If there are no fences with sheep or rabbit netting on them in your area, then it makes sense to build a fenced-in square (if you can manage to get the materials and ground). Into this square you can throw your dummies so that at least you can send your dog on a retrieve involving a fence that needs to be jumped. Whatever you do don't be complacent, use your imagination!

A good example of incomplete gundog training was once shown to me by a good friend who brought his five-year-old Labrador bitch with him when he visited me. This was a dog who was excellent in all forms of retrieving – with one exception. To my astonishment when walking around the loch near my home I discovered that the dog had never been swimming. My friend explained that in the area of England where he lived there were no waterways beyond the odd ditch, and he had never taken the trouble to take his dog to water.

By now your dog should look forward to his training outings so it is time to make him work that bit harder. Sit him in front of you, shoot the dummy over his head so that it goes directly behind him, then leaving him sitting, walk directly away from him in the opposite direction to where you have left the dummy. Call him to you by hand or whistle and, when he is halfway stop him on the whistle and give him the 'go back' command (using voice and hand), sending him back for the dummy. The distance of the 'go back' can be worked with him quite easily up to at least 200 metres.

A variation of the same exercise, which requires a large field, is to sit the dog in the middle of the field, shoot a dummy on either side of him, then walk about 100 metres away. After a short wait send the dog on the retrieve. Immediately blow the stop whistle. Once he has sat, wave him to retrieve the other dummy. Take the retrieve, make him sit and then send him to pick the dummy still in the field.

There are many other variations:

- Shoot a dummy into cover where the dog can only see the line of its fall, but not the exact location, then send him out on a retrieve.
- Shoot a dummy over a wall, or over water, into cover where it cannot be seen, and send the dog to retrieve it.
- Shoot three dummies in three different directions, one after the other, and then send the dog to pick two of them, retrieving the third yourself.

Continually strive to create new and challenging retrieves for your dog.

Advanced dummy retrieving is designed to prepare the dog for the next and much more difficult training – that of blind retrieving. So, the more preparation and the more you can smooth the way through your dog's education by a constant and steady increase in the difficulty and complexity of the tasks you put him to, the easier it will be for the dog to continue his development.

By this stage in his training, if you have been stretching the distance you send the dog for a retrieve, and the time you keep him waiting between shooting the dummy and sending him for it, you will have extended his capacity to mark and remember. The 'go back' command is a perfect example of quite how surprising some dogs' memories can be, and if it is done with a gradual increase in time and distance, your dog's mental capacity can be improved and developed.

A good example of this – though by no means rare or unusual – is a young dog which I am in the middle of training. A few months ago, if I dropped a dummy in sight of him and walked on with him at heel for much more than fifty metres, and waited too long (two or three minutes) he

*Introducing a Springer Spaniel to quartering in thick, game-rich bracken. Note how the trainer is ensuring that the dog stays close and under control at all times.* (JAMES DOUGLAS)

would already have forgotten. Yet now, walking around the loch near my home, I can stop him, making him sit, throw a dummy down, then walk in with him at heel for several hundred metres before telling him to sit. Standing in front of him you can see the anticipation in his face as he waits for the command to go back, which he does with unerring accuracy.

Yet even with a bright dog small obstacles that seem simple to us can surprisingly upset the canine mind. For instance, if you throw a dummy down and take the dog away with you on the – by now familiar – walking to heel, then cross a high wall and walk on for another fifty metres before sending him back, you can often find that the dog will run back to the wall and cast up and down the wall as though he has forgotten where the retrieve lies. The answer is to give him more practise at shorter distances until he is confident about crossing anything in his path.

Advanced retrieving is largely dependent on the facilities you have, whether it is a public park, farmland, woodland or seashore. Utilize cover and distance. Don't be afraid to send a dog on a retrieve, stop him half way and either move him to another retrieve or give him the recall command. Confidently remain in control of your dog and you will find these lessons easily learnt.

## Blind retrieves – is the nose working?

So far all retrieving and whistle-control work has been to prepare your dog for a long blind retrieve where he has no idea where the game is. Every gundog owner dreams of being at a shoot when he is asked to send his dog on some long and distant retrieve where a bird has fallen. To the astonishment and delight of the watching guns he can direct his dog – with a minimum of fuss – into the area of the fallen bird. Yet this ability is comparatively easily achieved if your dog's training has been consistently progressive, from puppyhood discipline to advanced dummy retrieving at a distance.

If your dog has become used to working far from you yet is still responsive to the whistle (and therefore under control) it is time to introduce him to blind retrieves. Like all other forms of gundog training it is always best to start off making things easy by working at close range. When you go to your training ground leave your dog sitting at the edge of the field and walk off any game that might be there. As you do this surreptitiously drop a dummy in long grass where the dog cannot see you drop it and return to him. Walk him into the wind and make him sit about twenty metres from where you know the dummy lies – upwind of him. Step back and give him the signal to fetch, giving him the line. If there is any hesitancy in him and remember that up until now he will have been used to a dummy being thrown or shot encourage him on with additional commands to 'fetch', using the arm signal and showing him the line. As he runs forward towards the dummy, give him the familiar 'steady' and you will find that with the aid of the dummy's scent he should find it quickly.

As soon as he picks it encourage him back and make a fuss of him. Continue this particular exercise over several training outings until you are sure he is quite confident in going out for this simple blind retrieve, either to left or right, according to your signal. But try at all times to use the wind to aid your dog in finding the dummy during these early stages.

The next step is to go back to your training area. Sit your dog and walk off the game (as before). Drop the dummy, go back and collect your dog, and make him sit as though you were going to send him for the hidden dummy. Then produce a second dummy and throw it clearly where he can see it, in the opposite direction from where the hidden one lies. Then, after a short wait, send him for the hidden dummy. His temptation, obviously, is to go for the one he saw falling. Do not allow this, and wave him to the hidden one. When he picks it, make a fuss of him and then, leaving him sitting, walk to the other dummy and let him see that you are retrieving it. The basic idea of these early blind retrieving exercises is to place in your dog's mind the confident knowledge that when you wave him into a retrieve, he will find one.

As your blind retrieving progresses, you will know how fast to move your dog on. Go to your training area and walk off the game. Put out several retrieves, throwing them into cover, over streams or walls, or wherever you can hide them. Then collect your dog and walk slowly around the circuit where you know the dummies are secreted. As you approach each hidden dummy, fire your starting pistol, giving the dog the drop-to-shot command. Carefully wave your dog out on a blind retrieve with the fetch command, giving encouragement when the dog returns with the dummy. By this time it is permissible to give him up to six blind retrieves in these outings. However, keep your eye on him and watch him carefully. If he becomes too fired up or over-exuberant on these retrieves, drop the number you give him back to two or three in each training session.

As your dog's competence on blind retrieves progresses, a good variation is to introduce him to retrieving tennis balls. Introduce him to the tennis ball as an object you want retrieved. To aid him in scenting, rub it through your hair, or under your arm. What you are doing is giving it a smell, which his keen nose will pick up. Once he understands that the tennis ball is for retrieving you can walk a circuit on your training ground and knock balls into cover with a tennis racket. Use them as blind retrieves.

The tennis ball technique is purely a variation of the shot dummy. Most people can lay their hands on an old tennis racket, and half a dozen balls are a great deal cheaper than half a dozen launcher dummies. Again, imagination is the watchword with blind retrieves. Hide them behind walls or throw them over streams. Then carefully work your dog on to the dummy by giving him the hand signals that he is now familiar with: go back, left, right, and call 'steady' as he nears the area you wish him to search.

Another technique to try is to shoot a dummy well to the right and in front of you. Then send the dog out for it on a sighted retrieve. As he nears the area, blow the stop whistle and allow him to collect himself as he sits and watches you. Then wave him away to the left, away from the dummy he has seen fall, and work him onto a hidden blind retrieve you have previously secreted. Or try this same exercise across water.

As in all other training, not only does practise make perfect, but by increasing the complexity of tasks and distances which you send him and expect him to work you will be highly rewarded as you see him learning to trust you and developing into the finished gundog.

## Advanced water work

Until this point your dog will have gained experience swimming in whatever water you have handy, retrieving in the natural course of his training. As your dog's proficiency, expertise and self-confidence in the water increases, you can move on to more advanced water work. However, make sure you do not lose sight of the fact that your dog is an athlete and he must be physically trained and ready for any form of advanced water work. If a dog is tired or fatigued in the field, you will not always notice because he can slow down or stop. Since few shooting activities call for a dog to move constantly without rest, you are less likely to see your dog flagging until he becomes very tired indeed. Certainly at the end of the day your dog may be so tired he flops down in the back of the car and goes immediately to sleep. But during the day he will have paced himself, taking short pauses to recoup his energy.

A dog swimming in water has no such recourse to take a rest. Unlike a human who can roll on his back and float if fatigued, a dog must keep swimming or will quickly get into difficulties. From the moment his body becomes buoyant when he leaves the shore, until his feet touch it on his return, he is active. Also, consider the cold. Water conducts heat twenty times faster than air and consequently you have a situation where the dog – depending on his physical abilities and condition – has a limited time in which it is safe for him to be in the water. Unlike a human a dog has no way of knowing when he must turn back or that he must keep sufficient energy in reserve to swim safely back to the shore.

With a bird swimming in front of him, a dog could swim on after it, determined to get it until he reaches exhaustion, with insufficient stamina to get him back to safety. Even if he does he may have seriously damaged his cardio-vascular system. So, if there is the slightest chance of you working your dog in water, you must get him in the right condition, working on his obedience in the water at the same time. In this way he should not only take directions, but will answer immediately if given the recall.

A dog's response to hand signal direction and whistle must be developed on land before you can safely and confidently start making him change direction in water. On land, for example, you will be able to throw or shoot a dummy to either side of him or straight over his head, keep him in

*Young Springer Spaniel entering the water with tremendous enthusiasm: the end result of a steady, patient introduction to water work.* (JAMES DOUGLAS)

a sitting position and give him the command to either go back or to retrieve left or right. You always have the insurance policy that if the dog goes in the wrong direction you can stop and redirect him. Part of his obedience training for hand signals on land is to send him to one side on a retrieve and halfway to it, stop and redirect him.

You can now start giving him the same commands in water, with a dummy shot out to the left or right, with the command to fetch. As he sets off in one direction, blow the stop whistle. Obviously he cannot sit in water, but he will – and should – respond to the whistle by slowing down and looking back at you. Then you wave him to the other dummy. If you have diligently worked on his hand signals on land retrieves, it takes only a short time before the dog learns the technique of treading water or swimming in a half-circle, watching you when given the stop whistle. Work on your hand signals in water at short distances, only progressing to longer retrieves as the dog becomes more expert.

For hidden water retrieves you find the real benefit of having given him a line direction. The technique in water is exactly the same as on land. Without your dog throw a dummy into a reed bed, where it cannot float or drift away. Then, returning with your dog to the bank where you know the retrieve is, line him up in the direction you want him to swim and give him the command to fetch. The first couple of times he does this in the water he will probably jump in, swim out, and then look back at you for direction. Do not give him directions that are too distant, but make it easy for him to find the hidden retrieve. Then as you progress in his water work you will be able to work him at ever-increasing distances.

One of the greatest problems faced by many gundog owners with water work is to get a dog to cross a river, canal or waterway, exit on the other side, and go up over the bank on a blind retrieve. Most dogs seem either reluctant or unsure of what the handler wants, and the only way to achieve success is to utilize water wherever possible as only part of the obstacle course between him and the retrieve.

Once the dog is working well on land to hand signals, going left, right or back, reduce the distance you want him to go after he crosses the water. Water brings another element or obstacle into the dog's mind, and if your dog is at the stage of working 100 or 200 metre retrieves on land, his across water retrieving at that time should not be more than fifty per cent of his land distance. Make it easy for the dog. Remember there is nothing more rewarding for you or your dog than the successful retrieve after a hunt, so avoid confusing the dog.

If you throw or shoot a dummy to the other side of a river where a dog can see it, send him across the water with the 'fetch' command and give him the line. As soon as he reaches the other bank stop him, make him sit and give him the hand signal and command to fetch again. As he grows used to taking the familiar hand direction, after crossing the water, you should have little difficulty in progressing on to hidden retrieves.

There is really no difference between sending your dog on a long retrieve across a field, stopping him on the whistle and directing him on to a hidden dummy, and sending him first across a river and then on a long retrieve. The only difference in technique is that you advance the land retrieves ahead of your progression across water retrieves.

If every time they enter water they bring out a retrieve, most dogs think that the retrieve will be found in the water. They show a marked reluctance to exit water, go up the opposite bank, over and out of sight, preferring to cast up and down the opposite bank. Even well trained dogs in this situation can appear oblivious to the handler's commands. But this will not be the case if you give the water no more significance than any other obstacle such as a wall, and give the dog plenty of experience crossing the water and taking hand signals. Always remember to stop the dog on top of the other bank, just before he goes out of sight, since this may be your last opportunity to give him a hand signal before he works out of sight.

A good example of this was a dog which belonged to man with whom I used to shoot. The dog had been well trained and was excellent, but had never really had any experience of crossing water and leaving it to get the retrieve. My companion shot a duck which landed neatly on the middle of a little island, about fifty metres from the bank of the small loch where we were shooting. It was obvious the bird had fallen dead and should have been a simple retrieve. The dog had not seen where the bird landed, and when it was sent out on a retrieve, took the line beautifully. He swam out with great enthusiasm, working the air and craning his neck to look for the bird he could not smell. The owner directed him nicely and eventually the dog actually waded into the shallows of the island, looking back at its owner for directions. But no matter how often he told the dog to go back, the dog was obviously convinced the bird was in the water and was reluctant to leave it. In fact the dog never did pick the bird, and had to be recalled.

I had a young dog who was a great deal less experienced but had had the benefit of more distance direction, and crossing water on retrieves, with only a small part of his water retrieves having actually been in the water. When the dog was recalled I sent my dog across and directed him on to the edge of the island where I blew the stop whistle, commanding the dog to sit. It looked back at me expectantly and I gave him the straight 'go back' signal. As he disappeared into the vegetation I gave him the 'steady' command to indicate that he was near the retrieve. The dog quickly reappeared with the duck and came straight back. My young dog was not as experienced as the older one, but had had the benefit of being directed across water, with obviously satisfactory results.

## Double retrieves

Possibly the most frustrating thing that can happen when you are shooting is for a dog on its way back with a retrieve, to break the line and go for another bird. Now whilst this is a relatively simple thing to avoid on land where you can command your dog to sit it is slightly more difficult in water. But if you have prepared the dog thoroughly with hand signals, and if he has learned the word 'no', then you should encounter few difficulties when you advance him to double retrieves.

Have two dummies ready to hand throw. Take your dog to the water's edge, tell him to sit and throw a seen dummy far out into the water. Line the dog up and send him for the retrieve. When he is half way back to you, throw the second dummy over his head. If he hesitates or makes the slightest movement to turn after the second dummy, immediately and sharply say 'no' and encourage the dog to come back to you. When he has exited the water – and you have taken the retrieve – after a short delay send him on a second retrieve.

It is also a great advantage if you have access to an older well-trained dog at this stage. After you have taken the first retrieve from your dog and told him to sit, send the other dog for the second retrieve, keeping the young dog in a sitting position, observing throughout, while the older dog gets the retrieve, brings it back and hands it over. Once the young dog has the idea that he must ignore the other dog, then you can progress to sending the older dog on the second retrieve while the young one is still retrieving.

Do not, however, try this initial double retrieve by sending the older dog too close to the young one. Keep the retrieve to one side. As the younger dog gains expertise it will soon become possible to throw the dummy straight over the returning dog's head and send the second dog on a retrieve, compelling both dogs to swim past each other within a few feet, ignoring each other.

## Simulated shooting – bringing out the gun for the first time

In all training exercises, as your puppy grows to a fully trained young dog, you should review the training techniques which will eventually build into a simulated day's shooting. So in your training sessions run over everything you have already taught your dog.

When it comes to the introduction of you carrying the gun, the dog is going to see another aspect of his work. You are going to look different. Instead of the familiar picture of you with your game bag, dummies, dummy launcher, starting pistol and lead, you are now going to be carrying an unfamiliar object. So again approach it sensibly. Set out on your training schedule, going over his lessons.

Walk him at heel, walk in a zigzag course, varying the speed and making sure that he drops quietly when you stop. Leave him sitting, walk away and return to him. Exactly as you introduced your dog to the sound of the starting pistol, use an assistant, who should walk fifty metres away and fire his gun in the air. Watch the dog for any sign of alarm. If he is concerned put off the exercise for another day. If not, move the gun ten metres closer each time it is fired until your assistant is standing beside the dog. It is unusual that a dog, which has already become used to the shot of a starting pistol and dummy launcher, will show any undue alarm at the sound of the shotgun. But is does not hurt to be cautious. The shotgun will make a louder, different sound to the starting pistol. You may think that at this advanced stage in the dog's training that I am being over-cautious, but I am a great believer in taking no chances when introducing a young dog to any new experience.

From now on, take your gun with you whenever possible. Use the shotgun frequently instead of the starting pistol in your dropping to shot lessons. You are, after all, now working towards a simulated day's shooting and a typical training period should contain all the constituent parts of his training to date. Each exercise should be a separate command and task to be performed. Try not to let them all run together too quickly.

## Dead game – keep it controlled

It is imperative that no gundog should ever be introduced to game as an object to be retrieved until all his training is largely complete. Until now all the work you will have done with him will have been under the controlled conditions of retrieving dummies. The fur and feather covering you have fitted is purely to get him used to the texture in his mouth, and he must not have been introduced to animals, alive or dead. He must think they have nothing to do with him, until you introduce him to dead game.

The reason for this approach is that your dog must be under your control at all times, be well mannered and versed in all forms of retrieving prior to the excitement that strong smells and dead animals encourage. A dog that has been introduced to the delights of carrying dead animals and has had his hunting instincts enhanced is going to find it a great deal more difficult when first brought to the rabbit pen – and expected not to give chase – if he has already carried game in his mouth. Therefore, the introduction to game is reserved until near the end of his training.

The best type of dead game to introduce your dog to, is the smaller, more easily carried specimens such as partridges or rabbits, eventually moving on to pheasants and ducks. Do not be tempted, no matter how strong and large your dog is, to ask him to retrieve hares, (unless they are very small) or geese, until he has become well experienced in carrying game. Large creatures such as hares and geese present a young dog with difficulties because of their weight and, in order to give himself better grip on the heavier game he must squeeze tighter. This can encourage a hard mouth. So continue with the principle we have so far employed throughout his training – make things as easy as possible whenever introducing your dog to a new experience.

If you can get rabbits which have been snared, so much the better, since it is not desirable – whatever you are going to use – that it should have blood on it. If you are using shot game it would be wise to sponge off any blood to avoid the

*Preparing to introduce this keen young Springer to retrieving cold game.* (JAMES DOUGLAS)

dog getting it in his mouth. If he does it may encourage him either to stop and lick off the wound or make him hesitant to pick it up while he stops and has a good sniff. You should also try to avoid rabbits which have been paunched and it is a simple matter to have a few of these in your deep freeze. Remember to let them thaw completely before you use them however, and if you are using fresh game, let it go cold first.

The technique is exactly as when you introduced him to the furred or feathered dummy. Take him to the training ground, throw a retrieve and send him for it. Take it and immediately throw a dead rabbit, sending him after that. As soon as he nears the rabbit, give him much encouragement, and call him in. Take the retrieve gently from his mouth with the word 'dead', give him much praise and put the rabbit away in your game bag out of sight. If he has a sniff at the rabbit before picking it, don't be surprised but do encourage him on, if necessary running away from him.

*Full of enthusiasm, the young Springer returns with the rabbit.* (JAMES DOUGLAS)

It can happen occasionally that a dog may be reluctant to pick game. Do not be concerned if your dog is one of these. Try again and if he is still reluctant, put it away for another day. Slot the retrieves into the beginning of his training schedule when you go out when he will be fresh and exuberant.

I do not recommend using the same dead specimen continuously and I much prefer to use one animal per retrieve, since the dog will have put saliva on the rabbit. But if you are short of game, you can re-use it. Try, however, to restrict yourself to a maximum of three retrieves with the same specimen.

Once the dog has been introduced to retrieving game, you can start to vary the retrieves, using as wide a variety of specimens as you have available. One bird I do not advise you to use with a young dog is the wood pigeon. They have particularly dirty, loose feathers, and there is nothing as discouraging for a dog as running out full of enthusiasm, bringing you a retrieve, and then standing with a mouthful of dry feathers which he has difficulty spitting out.

If you have a small dog you may find that some species require a little preparation until he gets used to picking and balancing game. Cock pheasants are easier for a small dog if the tail feathers are pulled out. This will stop him treading on them as he runs back to you. As I have previously said, geese can be difficult. Their long necks and large wings can end up tripping the dog as he tries to carry them. Let him become happy, relaxed and confident in his dead game retrieves before you gradually give him heavier specimens.

## Teach your dog how to take a line

While all gundogs have a natural ability to follow a scent line, this ability can be enhanced, nurtured and developed. The advantages of being able to follow a line are obvious, the most immediate being that up until now retrieves the dog has found have been from a single scent source – where the dummy has lain after it has fallen. Now, with the aid of a dead rabbit, we are going to develop the use of his nose and encourage him to work out scents.

While it is entirely permissible to use a piece of rabbit skin for this, I find that it is best to use the whole dead rabbit. The butt of a salmon rod, or a broom shaft with a couple of eyelets and a large fishing reel fitted to it, are ideal for this purpose. Tie the end of your fishing line to a rabbit's back leg. You are going to drag it backward against the lie of the fur, to give a marginally strong scent.

Go to your training area. Walk about twenty-five metres from the area of long grass where you intend to throw the rabbit. Throw it out and walk, paying the line out as you go. After you have walked about twenty-five metres, walk across at right angles to the line you have taken, and reel the rabbit in. It is imperative that you lay the rabbit line into the wind. Untie the rabbit and leave it in the long grass. You do not drag the rabbit behind you because your scent would intermingle with the rabbit's. It is much better to give the exercise that little bit of extra effort and lay a separate line of rabbit scent for your dog to follow.

*Springer Spaniel learning to hunt a line through thick cover.* (JAMES DOUGLAS)

*Giving a clear signal as the dog is sent for a retrieve.* (JAMES DOUGLAS)

Get your dog and work him into the wind. As he nears where you know the line begins he should start to show the tell-tale signs indicating he is on to a scent – nose closer to the ground, tail wagging, and general signs of excitement. Fire a shot, either from your shotgun or starting pistol. This will make the dog drop. Let him sit for a short time then give him the command to fetch and the line to follow. As he nears where you know the rabbit to be, encourage him by repeating 'steady' once or twice. When he picks the retrieve and brings it in, give him praise, take the retrieve, put it in your game bag and continue on.

## Summary

Your dog has now advanced to serious gundog work. He knows the basics and by the age of around eighteen months you will have taught him the refinements of what a good, well-trained gundog should know. These include:

- Directional hand signals – to right, left and back.
- Advanced dummy retrieving – two or three dummy retrieves; using the ground.
- Blind retrieves.
- Advanced water work –including multiple, blind and across water retrieves.
- Double retrieves – re-enforcing your control.
- Introduction to the gun.
- Introduction to dead game.
- Taking a line – scents and how dogs use scent.

Added to his vocabulary is:

- Go back

# 8

# EIGHTEEN MONTHS TO TWO YEARS

By this stage in your dog's education he will have progressed almost to the point of being fully trained, and with general obedience, work with directional signals, retrieving of dummies and cold game, he should be spot on. The only game he has seen will have been dead. It is now time to introduce him to the ultimate temptation – live game.

Let me emphasize that this is one particular aspect of your dog's training that can in no way be short-circuited. He must be absolutely reliable in all aspects of live game if you are going to avoid the ultimate nightmare of all gundog owners, the crime of running in. There is nothing more demoralizing to any field sportsman than a dog which gives chase. Some of the most potentially superb dogs I have seen have been rendered completely useless by the fact that as soon as live game appears in front of them they have a tendency to take off. It cannot be tolerated. It must never be allowed to happen, and if correctly approached, should never happen.

*It is essential that you never allow your dog to run in or to chase fur or feather.* (JAMES DOUGLAS)

Your dog should, by now, be 100 per cent reliable to the stop whistle and sitting on command. More importantly, you will by now have built a communicative understanding between your dog and you. He should be able to recognize your moods and intentions and should understand the inflections of your voice. You, in turn, should be experienced at reading your dog, observing all the signs that he gives when he is getting excited. But most important, this communications bridge, the bond which good gundogs and their handlers have, should be well established.

If you have worked diligently with your dog, if you have followed each stage in this book and made sure that each addition to his training schedule has been thoroughly and completely learned, then when you introduce him to live game, you should have an excellent control and communications line between you, and the rabbit pen should give you few problems.

## The rabbit pen (dropping to flush)

Gundogs should drop to flush. I prefer them to sit – rather than just stop – when game is flushed, since the action of sitting is, to my mind, more positive than simply stopping. In training a dog to drop to flush, the use of the rabbit pen is invaluable.

If you can construct a rabbit pen yourself, so much the better. The size is governed by the amount of ground you have available, and how much you can afford to spend. If these facilities are impossible for you, then contact a professional gundog trainer in your area and ask him if you can have access to his pen, explaining the reason why you need it. Most gundog trainers would be happy to encourage you. If there are no professional trainers with rabbit pens in your area, then approach an estate keeper and ask if you can use one of his release pens when it is not in use. Whatever type of pen you use, you must have in it half a dozen rabbits, and perhaps one or two pheasants, with their primary wing feathers pruned to stop them flying. Under these controlled conditions, where you know you can flush a rabbit, you will find it that bit easier than just working your dog in the open, in the hope that you can blow your whistle at the same time flushing a rabbit.

Take your dog on the lead into the rabbit pen and walk him at heel around the pen, until he sees a rabbit. Immediately the dog spots the rabbit tell him to sit. Repeating the word 'sit' take the lead off and walk around the pen, flushing the rabbit. Keep your eye on the dog and if there is the slightest indication that he is going to chase, command him to sit. If he chases a rabbit, blow your stop whistle, get after him, grab him and roughly drag him back to where he had originally been placed. Give him a shake and again command him to sit. Then repeat the process of walking up the rabbits.

The idea of this exercise is to make the dog quite used to sitting while all these temptations hop about within his sight. After a few lessons, once it is obvious the dog has the idea that it must not chase, when you next go into the rabbit pen, walk the dog around. In the case of a spaniel or pointer you can cast it out, but watch the dog carefully. The instant a rabbit bolts in front of the dog, blow the stop whistle. Allow the dog to sit, watching the game disappear, then go to him and make a fuss of him. Let him know you are pleased, then continue the exercise, giving him two more flushes.

Once our dog has experienced many trips to the rabbit pen over several weeks, he should be absolutely steady to game. Add in the variation of giving him a short retrieve with the hand-thrown dummy through the rabbit pen. Be particularly careful when you first introduce him to a retrieve in the pen that he doesn't suddenly succumb to the temptation – now that he is on his

*Using pheasant poults in a rearing pen to teach a young Labrador to remain steady in the presence of game.* (JAMES DOUGLAS)

feet and moving – of having a quick burst after something he may flush. So be ready with the stop whistle. However, if you have meticulously worked at keeping him steady in the pen, this should not arise.

Obviously, the rabbit pen has its limitations. Eventually the dog becomes familiar with the regime when he is taken into the pen and it is, after all, just to prepare him for the experience of flushing game in the field. But the pen is invaluable throughout a dog's life. I am a real believer in occasional refresher courses before the beginning of a shooting season. They sharpen a dog up and remind him that game is not for chasing.

If you have a spaniel that is sluggish and not really wanting to hunt (normally due to lack of hunting drive), take the spaniel into the rabbit pen and allow it to chase. Get it fired up then once it has the idea of hunting and chasing rabbits you must stop it chasing by putting extra emphasis on the stop whistle and getting after the dog in the pen when it does so. Smack him if necessary. Let him know chasing will not be tolerated. It may seem a bit contradictory to the idea of never chasing but it is the way that you can encourage hunting in an otherwise pottering spaniel.

At this stage in your dog's training it is time to take him out of the rabbit pen and let him experience wild game he is not prepared for. Go to an area where you know you will find rabbits. The best time to do this is early in the morning. Rabbits sit tighter early in the morning. Later in the day they are likely to bolt much sooner.

Working your dog into the wind, towards where you would expect a rabbit to sit, have your stop whistle ready, and the instant they flush, blow the whistle. In these early excursions in the field, don't wait to see if he sits when the rabbit bolts without the aid of the whistle. Have it ready to refresh his memory if he doesn't sit immediately. If there is the slightest temptation to chase, the best course of action is to return to the rabbit pen and give him further tuition.

An alternative to the use of rabbits, and one which I am keen on using is that of dizzied, or captive pigeons. The advantage of using a pigeon is that the dog cannot possibly chase it since the bird quite literally flies away. Contact a pigeon fancier and approach him – on bended knee – for the occasional loan of one of his least valuable birds. Explain to him that the bird will come to no harm, and obviously assure him that if it doesn't return you will be happy to reimburse him for the loss of the bird.

The dizzied pigeon technique is relatively simple to employ. Hold the bird gently in both hands and carefully push its head under one wing. Then holding it upside down move it gently in a circular motion for a minute. The bird will be stupefied as though in a trance, and will remain in this state for about ten minutes. Then lay it carefully in the long grass. Get your dog and work him into the wind, towards where you know the bird to be. Try to time your dog's arrival at the bird to about ten minutes. As the dog comes up to it, the bird – which has by now started to regain its equilibrium – jumps to its feet and flies away.

There is another method which I prefer, but which requires more effort on your part, does not involve the dizzying of the bird and puts you in much greater control of the exact second the bird flushes. You are also in better control of flushing the bird, either a few metres in front of the dog, or quite literally right under his nose. This is referred to as the 'buried pigeon'.

Dig a small hole in the ground, which should be large enough for a pigeon with one wing fully opened and deep enough for the bird, when standing on the bottom of the hole, to have its head about three centimetres below ground level. A piece of plywood, cut slightly larger than the hole, is slid over the top once the bird is in, with a long string (about thirty metres) fastened through a hole you have drilled in the wood. Remember to lay it out downwind. The bird will remain there perfectly safely until you work your dog towards the hidden bird.

As he approaches the secreted bird, pick up the string and pull the lid away from the bird, which should immediately fly skywards. As the bird flushes, blow the stop whistle. A little practise will quickly teach you how close to let your dog get to the bird before you flush it. You will also find that you can flush the bird right under the dog's nose. The bird flies back to its loft, completely unharmed, and can be used again and again.

Another obvious advantage of this technique is that since the bird is perfectly safely hidden, and you do not have the limiting time factor of the dizzied pigeon (which will only remain dizzied for a short period of time), you can put out several birds on a circuit. In this way you can more closely simulate an actual day's shooting, flushing the birds at your leisure.

## Scents

Since men began working with dogs, it has been take for granted that their more developed scenting powers allow them to follow invisible scent lines, which are beyond our ability to detect. But an understanding of what scent really is will help the gundog trainer to comprehend the many and varied problems your dog may have to face on any shooting day.

In scenting terms dogs fall into two categories: ground scenters and air scenters. The air scenting dogs, such as the GSP, will primarily follow scents which are above the ground, and this can be illustrated by the dog running with his head up. Ground scenters predominantly find their scents on the ground, and this is illustrated by the Labrador following a line, his nose skimming and searching close to the soil. However, although they may be masters at their own speciality, air scenters can follow a ground scent, and vice-versa.

Weather conditions play an important part in whether a scent is strong or weak. Whenever there is talk of gundogs and dog work, you will often hear the comment that it was a bad scenting day. This is not an excuse. There are days when scenting conditions appear to be ideal, the scent remaining for a considerable time after the passage of an animal or bird. On a windy day air scent will dissipate quickly. On a very hot day, the scent will tend to rise and disperse in the air currents. Obviously, in heavy rain a scent will be suppressed and quickly dilute. The best scenting conditions are crisp, cold days, with a light breeze to give the dog direction.

### What is scent?

Scent is made up of a variety of constituents. As your dog's nose becomes educated, and able to discern and filter the different smells, he learns how to discard the unimportant and unwanted smells and concentrate on the odours that guide him on the line taken. A bird or animal – whether it is a cock pheasant or a rabbit – has a distinctive odour and as it passes across or through vegetation, it will leave small scent molecules. It will add to the channel of smells disturbed leaves, broken grasses, small seemingly unimportant smells which all unite into a distinctive trail.

Most of us only ever come across the question of scent when our gundog is sent after a runner, and this is where the scent is likely to be much stronger. How, for instance, does a dog know how to follow a line of one particular wounded pheasant that may have run through cover which contains several other birds? It is because of the chemical group known a pheromones. We have all heard that a dog knows if you are afraid of it. This is quite true. The dog also knows if you are not

*The importance of scent to a gundog.*

*This experienced Labrador first winds the pheasant...*

*...then homes in to collect it...*

*...and finally brings it to hand to complete a stylish retrieve.*
(JAMES DOUGLAS)

afraid of it. It is given this information by the scent given off by your skin glands, over which you have no control. They register your mood, and the dog, with highly attuned scenting capabilities, instinctively knows whether the scent means fear, aggression, confidence or something else.

So the pheasant which has been pricked, which comes to earth with a bump, is giving off a distinctive odour of alarm, or fear. It is wrong to suggest that it is either the smell of the shot having struck the bird, or the smell of blood. I have heard both these suggestions, but neither has any scientific basis. A pricked bird seldom bleeds – at least for some considerable distance – but it does know that something is wrong and, as it runs off to hide, it obviously has some degree of anxiety, and this trail is easily followed by the experienced nose of a gundog.

A good way of seeing how obvious a smell channel is can often be witnessed as your dog becomes more experienced. Watch him as he nears the area where you have hidden a dummy. He will cast backwards and forwards into the wind. Sometimes, if the wind is swirling, he will show the distinct signs that he has smelt something and start to run towards the hidden dummy. Then he may stop, he has lost the smell, and cast backward and forwards again before he locates it, running along the invisible track to the hidden retrieve.

## 'The jigsaw is complete'

As I have said previously, you will have been building up your dog systematically over his training schedule, constantly going over everything that has been learnt to date as you add in each new aspect of his training. Now that your dog is dropping to flush and has reached this point in his training, he is fully trained. His education is complete, but he is still not a gundog – that only comes with experience. You can liken your dog to a university graduate, or an apprentice. Irrespective of how clever the individual is, regardless of how talented or adept at picking up education he is, it is the *experience* of working in the chosen profession that makes the student or apprentice complete.

In the case of your dog, it is the real shooting field that will give him the experience that will develop him, over a couple of seasons, into the complete gundog that you can be proud of. But there is much more that you can do to help your dog polish his skills, to hone his reactions so that he is sharp, responsive and obedient.

The best way of going about the final training of your dog, when you can consolidate everything you have taught him so far, is in a simulated shooting day. Leave your dog at home or in the car and set off with three live pigeons and have a dozen specimens of dead game in your bag – perhaps three rabbits and three pheasants. Lay out your set up, using your imagination, to give your dog as much variety as possible.

When you have secreted the retrieves and hidden the pigeons for flushing, return to your dog. To help you remember the exact location of the game it is a good idea to stick a small cane, sapling or twig near each hidden specimen, so that you have a guide to its location. There is nothing more annoying than discovering yourself unsure of exactly where you have left a hidden bird.

Dressed as though you were going for a day's shooting, and

*Introducing a young Labrador to game, seen here retrieving dead game through lush summer vegetation.*
(TERRY SCROGGIE)

*Even when the dog has fully mastered his lessons it is still important to keep polishing his skills in training sessions.*
(JAMES DOUGLAS)

carrying your gun, set off with your dog at heel. If he is a Pointer or Springer, you should be working him into the wind, in a nice tight and controlled pattern. Any wild game that you flush is a bonus and your dog should be 'bomb proof'. Using the game you have hidden means that you can set up your dog while you are still in control, working the dog through his training regime of walking to heel, quartering, dropping to whistle, staying where he has dropped when you fire a shot while you walk off and retrieving an imaginary piece of game. Return to him and either cast him out or walk him with you.

As you approach the first retrieve, try to slow down everything in your own mind so that each aspect of the shot and retrieve is perfectly executed, with no sloppiness from either you or the dog. Fire a shot when the dog has his back to you and make sure he drops. Then after a short wait, work him out on to the retrieve. As he comes into the area where you know the game to be hidden, remember to give him that verbal aid when he is nearing the vicinity by calling 'steady'. Take the retrieve, which should be nicely presented, put it in your game bag, give the dog acknowledgement, and work on.

If you have alternated the retrieves and the flushes, and if you have used your imagination on where you have hidden the dead game, you should have a retrieve from cover, from across water, over a wall – in fact anywhere the environment and your imagination will allow. When you have completed the circuit, you will have gone through his whole training regime and you will be able to see if there are any aspects of his training, any individual task, that needs some practise. Then you can concentrate on improving and sharpening him up.

If, on the other hand, you feel completely satisfied with all aspects of his work, don't allow yourself to become complacent, but continue to polish his training on a regular basis until the beginning of the shooting season, when wild game should supersede everything that has been organized and controlled so far. The type of training is based on the principle of an undisturbed and relatively painless progression from untrained puppyhood through to the working dog, and if you keep to the schedule, by this time in his training, both you and the dog should thoroughly enjoy your trips outdoors working together.

# 9
# TAKING YOUR DOG SHOOTING

Until the day you first go shooting your dog's training schedule has been arranged in such a way that he has been systematically working towards the event in an increasingly more authentic pattern, so that he is well prepared for the day when you first take him shooting. In many ways it may almost be an anti-climax. If he has had a thorough training he should take the first day's shooting in his stride, and any nerves will largely be your own.

No matter how well trained your dog is and how good your control of him is, it is important you are aware of what to avoid. It would be unwise to take your inexperienced dog on a formal shoot – or any shooting where there are likely to be several guns or dogs – unless you are not intending to shoot and can devote your attention to working the dog, giving him all your concentration, rather than trying to handle him while you shoot.

For his first day out it is a good idea to go with someone else who is a good shot. Leave your gun at home and concentrate on working your dog while your friend shoots.

You must, at all costs, avoid runners. Your dog will have to face the prospect of retrieving runners fairly soon, and there are a few simple but important guidelines to follow. Your dog must be made to drop to shot, and, no matter how tempted you are, do not allow a young dog to chase a runner until it is well out of sight (and preferably couched) before you send the dog after it. The dog, after all, does not know the difference between chasing a runner and chasing unshot game that runs away. Also, if the runner has run off and hidden, it gives your dog the opportunity to practise his ability in taking a line.

Wounded game that runs off and couches is more likely to stiffen up as it bleeds internally, is less likely to run off vigorously when the dog finally approaches. It is unfair to expect a young dog to know the difference between a fleeing animal which has been wounded, and a fleeing animal that it puts up as it works the ground. If you allow a young dog to pursue runners you are teaching the dog to chase and run in.

Runners to be avoided in particular, are pheasants. Anyone who has experience pheasant shooting knows the surprising ability some pheasants have for running great distances before hiding. Therefore, always try to stick to rabbits or game that is dead for your dog's first few shooting days.

Another important reason not to allow young dogs to go after runners is that until now your dog has been encouraged to pick game gently – to be soft-mouthed. If he is faced with picking a struggling animal, he can develop a hard mouth by taking a firmer grip than you would wish.

So tell your friend that if he is in any doubt that the quarry is dead, he should shoot it again. For this reason it is advisable to stick to ground with a healthy rabbit population. A pheasant which comes down and is a runner is a great deal more difficult to shoot again. It is also a waste to have to put more lead into such a desirable bird for the table!

*Gundogs and handlers gathered at the start of a day's shooting.* (JAMES DOUGLAS)

Each time a rabbit is shot, make sure your dog has dropped, and leave him in a sitting position if the rabbit is visible and an easy retrieve, and pick it yourself. Try to make sure that all these early retrieves are from rabbits which the dog cannot see lying dead under his nose. It is better to work him into a hidden rabbit and give both you and the dog plenty of time to work the ground.

Explain to your companion that since it is your dog's first day you intend to concentrate on him and that you would appreciate his help and understating. If he has a dog – unless it is impeccably trained – ask him if he would mind leaving it at home. It is foolish to take a young dog into the field if there is the slightest chance of a badly trained dog running in, perhaps taking game from the young dog, and generally competing with him.

You must, of course, accept that you will shoot in the company of other dogs at some time, and the correct way of doing so is simple. If you have a Pointer or Spaniel, and your shooting companion has a Retriever, you should let your dog work the ground, dropping to flush when game is shot. Now you are faced with a dilemma – which animal should be allowed to retrieve? The best course of action is to alternate the retrieve. Keep your dog sitting, go up beside him so

*A good, stylish retrieve from a young Spaniel.* (JAMES DOUGLAS)

you are standing fairly close, while the other dog goes for the retrieve. Then continue on your way, working the dog. When the next game is shot both dogs should be commanded to sit and then, standing well back from your companion and his dog, give your dog the command to retrieve. You stand away from the other dog because some dogs are reluctant to bring a retrieve too close to another dog, for fear of it being taken away. So stand well to one side and take the retrieve. In this way you will prevent the dog thinking that every retrieve is automatically his property, thus enhancing his good manners.

If you have a Retriever and you companion has either a Spaniel or Pointer, just reverse the procedure, keeping the dog working with you, under control, as he watches the other dog working, and alternate the retrieves. I should stress, however, that if your companion has a dog which you are doubtful about, you should not work your dog or expose it to the bad habits of the other dog. More good dogs are ruined by bad examples being set to them in the field than by anything else.

Earlier I drew a parallel between a young dog and a student getting their education, pointing out that experience is what makes a gundog. You must remember that the experiences of the first season's work are largely what will govern your dog's attitude and behaviour in the field in the years to come. All experiences in the field during a dog's first season should be regarded as confidence building. Common sense must prevail, for after so much hard work you should be cautious if you are to prevent your dog being fired up, with the subsequent lack of control and lack of sharpness in his reactions.

## Picking-up

Not for nothing do those who are keen on dog work – and who compete in trials – spend much time picking-up, for I know of no better experience in the shooting field to tighten up you and your dog as a working team. It is picking-up over a season which, more than any other activity, will teach you to read your dog's reactions, to fine tune your combined work together, and your control over the dog in a whole variety of difficult situations. Some people who are more used to shooting, have a tendency to feel that picking-up is a humble exercise, and this is very silly. Picking-up is an integral part of the serious dog handler's year, and opportunities should be sought out and capitalized on.

Approach the head keeper, or shoot captain of your nearest large shot, and explain to him that you have a young dog you would like to give the opportunity of picking game. Whilst most shooters are usually only too delighted to have someone with a good dog, make it clear that it is picking-up you want to do, and not beating, since while picking-up is an excellent aid to training, beating can have the distinctly opposite effect. The Spaniel who has never experienced the exhilaration of other dogs, abundant game, and the general commotion of beaters and guns, is almost guaranteed to become over-heated, and as soon as you enter the covert and he is cast he is likely to be tempted to draw you that bit further. Aided by the general excitement from the other dogs, the dog can – to the owner's dismay – appear to have completely forgotten all his training as he charges about, out of control. So if beating is all that is offered to you, do not be tempted to use a young and inexperienced dog, unless it is kept on the lead and is taken along as a spectator, not a participant.

When you arrive on the day to pick-up, it is well to go through the following few formalities, which will not only single you out as being entirely serious about your dog work, but will also give you superior results with your dog.

*Dogs should remain quietly in the back of the car prior to a shoot. These Irish Setters show good discipline as they wait for the start of a field trial.* (David Hudson)

If you have an estate car, open the back of the car, and tell your dog to sit. Leaving the back of the car open, with the dog remaining where it is, join the other beaters and pickers-up for the day. Introduce yourself to the head keeper and let him know of your arrival. Keep an eye on your dog, who should remain sitting in the back of the car.

A typical scene on such occasions is one of relative confusion, as the guests, beaters and pickers-up arrive. There is the inevitable jumble of dogs charging this way and that, sniffing each other, lifting their legs against every car wheel and fence post, and generally enjoying some communal canine fun. These dogs are, at this time, out of their owners' control and this is when the general excitement of the day starts to build within the dog. Much better to keep your dog sitting quietly in the back of the car until the shoot is ready to move off, when you get the dog and keeping him at heel and under control. Go to your allotted position.

If you do not have a car which allows you to leave the dog sitting in the back, or if your dog is excitable, then you should keep him on the lead as you introduce yourself to the other pickers-up. What you are trying to avoid is letting your dog – even for the shortest time – be out of your control.

A perfect example of this was illustrated by a gentleman who bought a dog from me. This dog was extremely well trained and 100 per cent reliable. As a personality he was calm and quiet with a complete lack of any nonsense, drawing his pleasure from working well. He had experienced two seasons as my own dog and it could be fairly claimed that he was exceptional in every way.

His new owner telephoned me several times after he had taken over the dog to tell me how pleased he was with him. He was shoot captain of a large and exclusive pheasant syndicate, and, quite simply, had to have the best dog, free from vices and beyond all form of criticism, since it fell to him to have to order other guns to leave their dogs behind if he felt they were not up to scratch.

After he had the dog a few months into the shooting season he sought my help with a minor problem which was developing. Apparently when sent on a retrieve the dog had, on one or two occasions, deviated and run to the next dog working on a parallel retrieve and had a quick sniff, before resuming his work on a command from his owner. I found this behaviour puzzling as I knew that this dog had never before been tempted to commit even this seemingly small misdemeanour.

After questioning the fellow about his routine I recognized the danger area. Although his home was less than an hour's drive from the shoot, when he arrived he thought it only fair the dog should be let out of the car to relieve himself. So for that short period of perhaps ten minutes or so, while the owner was engaged in conversation with the other guns, he was allowing his dog to move freely amongst the other dogs, joining in the general mêlée and indulging himself in the delights of a communal sniff. Unwittingly the new owner, having allowed his dog this small freedom, had taught him to pay attention to other dogs that came into his immediate proximity. I suggested he stop allowing the dog to intermingle in this way, and the problem stopped.

Walk with your dog to the peg or area you have been told to put yourself. Place yourself well behind the gun. If you are on a grouse moor either stand right by a butt or go well back out of shot. Remember that grouse fly close to the ground and that guns regularly turn to shoot at birds behind the butts. With high driven pheasants – particularly if the shot is on hilly countryside – it may be necessary for you to stand 100 metres behind the gun. Make sure he knows where you are. The actual distance between you and the gun will be dictated by the type of shooting and configuration of the ground.

*Driven shooting: the Cocker Spaniel waits expectantly at the peg as a shot is taken…*

*...returns with a cock pheasant
through thick cover...*

*...and settles down beside its proud
owner ready for the next retrieve.*
(Terry Scroggie)

Some people prefer to let all the birds
fall and then wait until the drive is over
before picking the game. I prefer to work
the dog on each bird as it falls. You get into
the habit of working your dog on a retrieve
while you count the birds that fall behind
the gun. Pay particular attention to strong
runners, birds that may be shot on one
wing and are far from dead, taking note in
which direction they have gone. Then as
soon as the drive is over, pick these birds
first. The possibility of encountering strong
runners is the reason for not taking a young
dog picking-up too early in his shooting
career. In the case of some runners it may
even be necessary to get your dog away to
it immediately, though this should only be
done with an experienced dog.

If you are picking-up on a shoot where a lot of birds are expected to be shot, it is no bad thing to take paper and pencil with you. Mark the top of the page with a circle, (indicating your gun) and further down the page another circle (indicating you). Then, as each bird falls, show the location with a small cross. This avoids confusion and means you have a greater chance of picking every bird. When you are picking-up, if you notice another dog is obviously on the same retrieve as your dog, stop your dog immediately and call him in. Otherwise you risk a tug of war.

At the end of the day remember to thank the keeper. He has, after all, done you a favour, and if you have played your part in the day's proceedings and your dog has behaved, then both of you are assured of being invited to subsequent shoots.

## Wildfowling

The one area of retrieving where it might occasionally be necessary for you to get your dog away speedily on a retrieve, rather than keep him sitting for a short spell before being sent out, is that of wildfowling. Water birds which are wounded have an alarming ability of being able to dive right in front of a dog, to reappear some twenty metres further on, and can cause a young dog to swim around and around in cold water on the futile pursuit of a bird which he has little chance of retrieving. At the same time he is burning up much-needed energy. So if you are shooting geese or duck, and a bird comes down that you think may not be dead, get the dog away quickly. In many cases a wounded bird – a goose for example – will often appear stunned for a few seconds after it has hit the water, before it regains its equilibrium and, on seeing the dog approach, will start to dive. Get your dog away immediately so he can be on to the bird before it starts to dive.

If you send a dog to retrieve a bird which starts to dive, and your dog starts to swim after it, you will see the benefit of having spent so much time doing advanced water work with dummies. In every shooting man's career there comes a time when he must decide whether it is best to lose a bird, allowing it get away wounded, than to risk his dog swimming endlessly back and forward in freezing water until he becomes exhausted and could drown. It is for that very reason you should have been diligent in the control of your dog, particularly when calling him off a retrieve. If, however, you have to put your dog on a retrieve quickly, sometimes even before the bird has hit the water – as may be the case if you have seen a goose coming down with one broken wing – then make the next two or three retrieves well controlled. Keep the dog sitting for several minutes before you send him on a retrieve, so you re-enforce control.

If you are faced with a situation when you must call your dog off a retrieve and leave a wounded bird, then you owe it not only to the bird, but to the good name of field sportsmen, to return the next morning and search for the bird. It will often be found dead, or at least a lot less active than in the previous evening's flight.

When shooting over floodwater, always check for submerged fences, which can be seen as the line of the fence comes out of the water. Either work you dog from an area where he is not going to encounter a submerged fence or if necessary, do not shoot, since a dog --no matter how experienced – when swimming in water (particularly if it is dark), has no way of knowing how to negotiate a fence which he comes against.

It makes good sense that you always pay attention to your dog's physical condition, and the little extra effort it requires to towel him dry at the end of the day will bring its own rewards. Do not expect a dog, irrespective of how tough and hardy you think he is, to have worked hard on a

*A fine retrieve from water as this Cocker Spaniel swims ashore with a duck...*

*...and hands it over to the owner.* (TERRY SCROGGIE)

cold rainy day and then to have endured either a wet journey home or being put into a kennel, wet and cold, without running the serious risk of the conditions which can be brought on later years with such lack of consideration.

Always dry your dog before putting him away for the night. If you have travelled by car to a shoot, dry him before you put him in the car. If it is cold, or you expect him to be wet and cold, the sensible, caring owner will take with him a nourishing snack, which he can feed the dog from the back of the car.

I have a large bag which has a drawstring around the top. The bag is sufficiently large to put my dog inside with the drawstring pulled loosely around his neck. In this way the dog remains warm, the moisture comes out of his coat and is absorbed by the bag during the journey home. This indulgence is entirely for the dog's benefit, but it does have the added bonus of keeping the car clean!

## Beating

Beating is a vital part of gundog work on shoots everywhere and there is always a place for a good, well-controlled beating dog. The beating line is also, as we have already seen, a minefield for the young, inexperienced dog with the excitement of scent, of game running and flying ahead of him, of other dogs working around him, of shots sounding and birds falling, of beaters shouting and blowing whistles for their own dogs, all combining to tempt him to forget his training and run wild. For all these reasons it is essential that you are extremely cautious when first entering your young dog into the beating line. That said, working as a beater can be great fun for you and your dog and is often a way to get involved with your local shoot with a view to going on to other things such as picking-up or shooting.

The work that is required from a dog in the beating line is simple enough in theory. His job is to work ahead of his handler, hunting out and flushing any game that is on his section of the beat. The difficulty for the handler is not generally one of getting the dog to do the job, but rather that of getting him to do it while properly under control when there is so much temptation for him to misbehave. Many handlers – even those whose main interest is working their dog as a beater – prefer to give the dog plenty of experience in retrieving before they allow him anywhere near the beating line. A full season, or even two seasons, picking-up would not be excessive so that you are quite confident of the dog's steadiness and your own control over him before you lead him into temptation.

The work that the beating line has to do can vary considerably depending on the type of shoot. Low ground shoots with pheasant as the main quarry are probably the most common, though even the ubiquitous pheasant shoot can vary a great deal between one place and another. The keeper on a big, commercial shoot, where the guns are expecting a bag of several hundred birds in the day, is likely to want the beaters to move through his coverts or game crop in a very quiet, controlled manner. There will be a big head of game in front of them and the aim is to flush the birds gradually, in twos and threes, and at all costs to avoid a mass flush that puts several hundred birds on the wing at the same time. Quite often much of the drive will be taken up with blanking in – walking the birds through the covert to a flushing point – and in this case it is essential that your dog stays close by you and doesn't press the birds too closely as they run in front. Given the choice a pheasant will usually prefer running to flying and a beating line can move pheasants quite

*Beating is great fun for the experienced gundog. Here the beaters are receiving their instructions between drives.* (DAVID HUDSON)

a distance provided that the dogs are properly controlled.

When the flushing point is reached your job is likely to be as much to prevent the birds from breaking back through the beating line as it is to actually get them on the wing. One or two steady dogs, or perhaps the keeper himself without any dogs, will be charged with the task of pushing the birds out and over the line of guns. Only when the majority of the birds have flown are you likely to be asked to send your dog in to hunt out the last few from where they have hidden. Indeed, on many commercial shoots the beaters will be withdrawn from the covert, no matter how many birds are left, once the keeper judges that the guns have had their allotted amount of shooting.

This type of shoot can be a good place to start giving your dog experience in the beating line, but only if you are very confident of your control over him, or are prepared to keep him on a lead. A single dog going out of control and rushing into the middle of a big bunch of pheasants can completely ruin a drive, and if your dog does this you are going to be very unpopular. The chances of a second invitation will be slight to say the least. If you are well on top of him though, it gives you the opportunity to let him see pheasants running without losing his head, to work alongside other dogs and to hone his hunting skills in the field.

At the other end of the shooting spectrum is the little local shoot where a much smaller bag is anticipated and the coverts hold only a small head of game. Here the emphasis is much more on the hunting ability of your dog and his skill at finding birds that may be tucked tightly into the undergrowth and are reluctant to get out and fly. On the big shoot it is neither here nor there if a couple of dozen pheasants tuck down in the bushes and are missed by the beating line, but on a small shoot a covert may only hold a couple of dozen birds in total.

Unfortunately, it is on these smaller shoots where you are liable to find yourself in company with dogs that work with little or no discipline from their owners. In terms of the requirements of the shoot this may not matter as long as the birds are flushed and sent over the guns, but it can be catastrophic for training purposes if your dog decides to join in the free-for-all with them. Make sure that you keep him working close by you and strictly under control at all times, dropping him whenever a bird gets up, keeping him well within your limits of control, and perhaps bringing him in and making him walk at heel from time to time. The aim is to ensure that he understands that, whatever the other dogs may be doing, he is still working for you and not for himself.

Working through game crops such as kale can be particularly testing for the handler because the height of the cover means that he cannot see his dog at all once he has been cast off. Until you are completely confident in your dog's discipline and steadiness I would advise strongly against letting him loose in the sort of cover where he will be out of sight for the whole drive. Sugar beet or turnips are a better proposition because in these you can usually see exactly what the dog is doing at all times and also have a good view of the other dogs and what they are up to. Some dogs get very excited when they first hunt through roots, possibly because of the swish of the tops as they race through them, but experience usually calms them down. The temptation to chase is greater in root fields than in higher cover because the dog can often watch the birds from the moment they are flushed right up to when they pass over the line of guns. In woodland or kale the birds are often out of sight within a few wing beats.

If you are able to get to the grouse moors during the summer and early autumn you should be able to find work for your dog as a member of the beating line. The distances covered by the beaters during a driven grouse shoot can be vast so both you and your dog need to be pretty fit if you are to cope, particularly if you are working under a blazing August sun.

A grouse moor can be a good place to introduce a young dog to beating for several reasons. The heather is short enough for you to be able to see exactly what your dog is doing at all times, and being out in the open should mean that there is a steady breeze to assist him in his quartering. The beaters on a grouse shoot are usually spread across a wide front, so the other dogs in the line are far less likely to interfere with your own dog than when they are working right alongside him in the close confines of a pheasant covert.

In many ways the handler with a young dog can treat a grouse drive as an extended training session while still doing the job for which he is being employed. Sending the dog out to right or left, recalling him, dropping him on the whistle and even bringing him to heel for a few minutes to calm him down if he seems to be getting overwrought will help to reinforce his training yet, provided you don't overdo the walking at heel, he will still play his proper part in the shoot.

In the open spaces of the moors most dogs will naturally pull out a good bit further from their handlers than when working in cover. Letting your dog work over a wider front should not be a problem as long as you ensure that he remembers that you are still in charge by turning him and recalling him from time to time rather than simply giving him his head and letting him work to his own rules.

# Rough shooting

The term 'rough shoot' can be applied to many different types of shooting, on moorland or marsh, woodland or farmland, but it is generally applied to the sort of shoot where the dogs are expected to play a dual role, both hunting and retrieving. For many sportsmen there is nothing as satisfying as working their dog through a likely piece of ground, watching as it hunts out its quarry, flushes it for the shot and then performs a retrieve. Bags are usually modest on the rough shoot but the sport can be absolutely first class for both dog and gun.

The rough-shooter's dog has to be versatile enough to do everything required of a gundog. A typical rough shoot, with four or five friends taking part could involve walking up pheasants from a field of roots, shooting rabbits as the dogs flush them on a bracken bank, hunting out a hedgerow for pheasants and rabbits, wading through a snipe bog, organizing a couple of impromptu drives from woodland, and then ending the day flighting ducks as night falls. You might go rough shooting in a party of seven or eight guns or there could be just you and your dog.

A rough shoot is not the best place to introduce a young dog to shooting. The excitement of hunting closely followed by the chance of a retrieve can easily go to the dog's head, especially if you are concentrating on your shooting and don't have your mind on your dog. If rough shooting is your chosen sport I would strongly recommend that for your first several outings with a young dog you leave the gun at home and let others do the shooting while you concentrate fully on what your dog is doing. You will be more than repaid in the years to come.

A lot of the challenge in rough shooting comes from the variety and the uncertainty of the work. When you set your dog off to work through a stand of young trees say, or a meadow overgrown with brambles, you are never sure just what he will find. Pheasant and rabbit of course in most places, snipe and woodcock if the ground is suitable, perhaps a hare or the odd partridge, a pigeon swooping out of the fir trees, maybe a grey squirrel dancing through the branches or an unwary crow that glides overhead.

A rough shooting dog needs to be adaptable. One minute he may be bashing through thorns and brambles and the next be splashing through the reeds and rushes of a snipe bog. On a stubble field he will be expected to quarter his ground quickly and methodically, using the wind to dictate his pattern, and then he may be hunting out a hedge bottom or a ditch that needs no actual quartering but may require him to push out well in front of the guns and then work his way back to them to try and ensure that a wily cock pheasant doesn't simply race to the far end of the hedgerow and then rise well out of range.

*English Springer Spaniel with the fruits of its efforts after a day's rough shooting.* (James Douglas)

It is on the rough shoot that the HPR breeds can be seen at their best. In America they are sometimes referred to as Versatile Hunting Dogs and that title neatly sums up their work. A good HPR will be as happy quartering the stubble field as he will be rooting out the rabbits from the hedge bottom. They are especially useful for the man who likes to go shooting with just a dog for company since, with their ability to point game rather than flushing it straight off, they can work a much wider front than a Spaniel.

Care is needed if you are working an HPR on a rough shoot or in a beating line where there are other dogs at work. It doesn't take a Spaniel long to realize what it means when the HPR comes on point and unless the other dogs are very well controlled by their handlers they are liable to nip in and flush game from under the pointing dog's nose. This is almost guaranteed to make him unsteady.

## Grouse shooting

Grouse shooting is so different from low ground shooting that it merits a section all to itself. We have already looked at working your dog in the beating line on a grouse moor, but you may be there as a gun rather than as a beater, or working an HPR, Pointer or Setter.

Shooting driven grouse is one of the best, and most expensive, forms of shooting available. If you are fortunate enough to be invited to a driven grouse shoot as a gun you will find one or two differences from the more usual driven pheasant shoot. Grouse naturally fly low, hugging the ground as they skim across the heather. Because of this the guns in the butts have to take great care not to swing through the line and endanger their neighbours. There are few sights more exciting than that of a covey of grouse racing towards the butts and every gun will have his or her full attention on the covey. Shots will certainly be fired in front of the butts as the birds approach and in many cases the guns will turn and shoot behind as they depart. Towards the end of the drive it is normal for a horn or a whistle to be sounded to signal to the guns that no more shots are to be taken in front because of the risk of hitting a beater and from then all shots until the end of the drive will be behind the butts.

It is essential that your dog stay in the butt with you, (or close beside the butt if room is limited) until the signal is given to end the drive. Under no circumstance should you send him for a retrieve until you are certain that no more shots will be fired. The speed at which grouse approach the butts, allied to their ground-hugging flight and the general excitement of a grouse drive means that any dog wandering about around the butts during the drive is in very real danger of being peppered with shot.

Once the drive is over and it is time to pick up it is essential to try and keep tabs on which birds have been picked – not always as easy as it seems because your neighbours' birds may be mixed in with yours, the beaters' dogs will probably pick up any that they come across as they approach the butts, and some of the grouse will be runners and not lying where you marked them down. Nevertheless, you should do your best and ensure that the pickers-up know if there are any birds still to pick when you are asked to move off for the next drive.

Walking up grouse is similar to working in the beating line, with the obvious difference that now you will be carrying a gun and looking to shoot the birds as they rise. You will need to keep your dog a little closer in than when beating so that the birds are in range when they are flushed and also to ensure that he is not in the line of fire from the guns on either side of you. Make sure that you keep in line with the rest of the guns and neither lag behind nor push on in front. It is usual for the line to be stopped whenever a grouse is shot so that it can be retrieved and these breaks offer a brief – and usually welcome – rest for dogs and guns alike.

Working a Pointer on the moor is a different game altogether. Shooting grouse over a Spaniel means keeping the dog close enough to the guns for them to be in range of any grouse that the dog flushes. Although an experienced dog handler can usually 'read' his dog well enough to be aware when the dog has picked up the scent of birds and have a few seconds warning that the chance of a shot is imminent, shooting over Spaniels always involves carrying your gun loaded and ready to fire as soon as the grouse rise. When the dog is a Pointer, Setter or one of the HPR breeds there should always be plenty of time to get ready to take a shot.

Shooting over pointing dogs is a completely different branch of the sport to walking up birds over Spaniels. This is an important distinction that is sometimes misunderstood by sportsmen. You should never work a Pointer in front of a line of guns as if he was a flushing dog. Walking in line behind a Pointer is confusing for the dog and can be dangerous if grouse are flushed between the guns and the dog as can happen on a downwind beat. If you are shooting over a Pointer the proper way to proceed is for the whole party to walk together a few yards behind the dog handler and to leave their guns empty until the dog points.

Any half-decent pointing dog should get out and quarter over a front of several hundred metres when working on a grouse moor. To anyone who has not seen pointing dogs at work it

*Flat-coated Retriever working on the grouse moors.* (JAMES DOUGLAS)

*Edward Hoy (aged 12) picking up at the grouse with a Flat-coated Retriever.* (JAMES DOUGLAS)

may seem that they must inevitably flush grouse far out of range of the guns, but in the early part of the season when most dogging work takes place the grouse will usually sit tightly enough to give the guns plenty of time to get across to the point before they take to their wings.

When a dog points two guns should go forward with the dog handler and take up position ten to fifteen metres on either side of the dog and perhaps a few metres ahead of him. Once the guns are ready the handler will send the dog in to flush the grouse. The whole covey may get up together but this is not always the case, so once the first shots have been fired the guns should reload. Then the dog will be sent on to clear his ground and put up any grouse that have stayed behind. Only when the dog shows by his behaviour that there are no more live birds crouched in the heather should you think about sending in the retrievers to collect the shot birds.

If you are working an HPR you may want him to handle the retrieving work as well as finding the birds for the guns. Pointers and Setters are not usually expected to retrieve in Britain, though most will if given the chance. No matter whether the pointing dog is also the retriever or whether you have specialist retrievers along to handle this side of the work, you should make sure that the ground has been cleared and that the guns are stood down before sending in the retriever. If your dog is an HPR this clear break between bird finding and retrieving helps to curb any problems that might arise if the dog is tempted to run in when he sees birds falling ahead of him.

# 10
# PROBLEMS AND SOLUTIONS

## Aggression

There is nothing worse than an aggressive dog. Most people do not know how to handle, control or respond to a dog that starts to show aggressive tendencies. A dog that becomes aggressive does so for several different reasons – fear, nervousness, defending its territory, dominance, or simply the dog has a mental problem and is just aggressive. Whilst this book is about training gundogs – a group of dogs not normally associated with aggression – it can occur with gundogs also. It is important that the trainer knows how to assess what is causing the behaviour and how best to tackle it.

Aggression – particularly extreme aggression – can best be explained if we first look not at gundogs but at a breed more commonly associated with aggression, the German Shepherd.

When the police initially assess a German Shepherd as a potential police dog, they break them into three categories:

- The first is the sort of canine personality which likes people and has no aggression whatever, they just want to lie in front of the fire. This sort of dog would never make a good police dog since it is more likely to lick you to death and has no prey drive.
- At the opposite end of the scale is the dog that has such a short fuse that given the slightest opportunity he would bite a human. This sort of dog has no future as a police dog, is highly dangerous and is better being put down.
- Then there is the dog in the middle ground that is prepared to stand its ground when necessary, who has self-confidence and can be trained to be reliable, able to go amongst the public without representing a threat – unless called upon to do so. This category is so rare that one top British police service finds that, on average, out of every hundred canine candidates only three ever become operational police dogs.

Irrespective of the breed of dog, the approach should be the same. Obviously handling a small aggressive Spaniel is easier and less intimidating than trying to deal with a German Shepherd. However, any dog that is likely to bite must be taken seriously and the reason for the dog's aggression identified and dealt with without delay.

Apart from specifically trained dogs such as some police dogs, or dogs that guard sensitive military installations, it is completely unacceptable for any dog ever to bite a person. Any owner of an aggressive dog must realize the responsibility they have to the rest of the community, and anyone who keeps an aggressive dog who subsequently bites anyone, is as guilty as the dog.

A dog that is afraid or nervous can often be brought out of the state by being carefully exposed to what is causing its fear or alarm. This could be traffic, people or strangers. There is a fine balance here and the trainer must use both intelligence and patience. If the problem is simply unfamiliarity – fear of the unknown – the trainer should gently take the dog on a lead into the vicinity, (but not too close to the cause of the dog's alarm), comfort the dog and let him see that there is nothing to worry about. If the dog shows severe fright take him away and try again another day.

I once had a black Labrador dog brought to my kennels by a friend who is an experienced amateur gundog trainer and who is prominent at the top level of field trials. Indeed he is a Class A trials judge. A busy professional, his all-consuming hobby is his gundogs. The dog was two-and-a-half years old, big, powerful and handsome. I had seen him picking up at shoots and in gundog tests, where he had acquitted himself well. My friend decided that the dog was never going to make the top echelon in trials, though he would make a first class shooting dog, and asked me to sell him on his behalf.

When my friend delivered the dog I put him into a kennel. After he had gone I went into the kennel block to have a look at the dog and was surprised to find he was hiding under his sleeping platform. All I could see in the kennel were two glittering black eyes staring out from the dark, accompanied by a deep-throated growl. When I started to open the gate the growling became more aggressive. It was obvious to me that the dog was frightened. Had I been stupid enough to go in and push my luck I would have been inviting a confrontation and risked being bitten.

I put a little food into the kennel and left him alone till the next morning, I was expecting him to be more relaxed with me. I was wrong! He growled more ferociously than ever. My first inclination was to phone my friend and ask him to take his dog away. But my curiosity at the behaviour – and my ego – got the better of me. There was no way I was going to admit that I could be beaten by a dog.

For the next few days I washed the kennels in the morning as quickly as I could, ignoring the growling coming from under the sleeping platform. Then from outside the kennel I threw tiny pieces of meat to land just in front of the dog's nose, which he cautiously ate. I repeated this exercise several times a day. That was the only food he got. When I fed the other dogs the Lab only got a few tiny scraps of meat. In fact the amount of meat he was eating in the day was more than adequate, but spread across the whole day.

By the end of the week the dog associated me with food, although he was still suspicious of me and what I might do to him. When I was near him I spoke in a quiet, soothing tone. In the second week I started throwing the meat to land half way between the dog and myself, compelling him to come towards me. After another couple of days the dog was picking the meat up from between my feet. If I made any sudden movement he immediately dashed back under the sleeping platform, growling. By the end of the second week I was able to go into the kennel beside the dog and he would allow me to stroke his head, all the time watching me with suspicion. But he was obviously becoming less afraid of me.

I eventually slipped a lead over the dog's head and led him out of the kennel. He was fine, he quickly relaxed with me and turned out to be a super companion and working dog.

After I had ironed out the problems with this dog I questioned my friend about what had been the dog's routine prior to him coming to me. I found out the reason the dog had been so aggressive.

My friend was a busy professional man, whose principal hobby was training and competing with his gundogs. His routine was the same each day. On returning from his office, he would change his clothing, put the dogs in the back of the car, and drive to his training ground. He would work the dogs, put them back in the car, drive home, put the dogs in the kennel, feed them, and go into his house. I was amazed when I found out that my friend's interest was purely in working the dogs, he had very little interest in the dogs themselves. He showed them no affection, and had never humanized them in any way. They had never been in a house, and had never been touched by any human being, other than to have the lead put around their neck, or a cuff round the ear when things went wrong. The dog was completely confused by me trying to befriend him and reacted by showing aggression.

Once I convinced this dog that I meant him no harm, and indeed that I liked him, he opened up and became a really delightful companion His was simply a classic case of a dog showing aggression out of fear. Once he realized there was no reason to be afraid everything turned out fine.

There are, however, other reasons for aggression and it is important that the trainer identify the reason why the dog's behaviour is as it is before starting to attempt to deal with the problem.

Assuming that there is nothing mentally wrong with the dog there can be several reasons why a dog might be aggressive. The most common one is that the owner is giving the dog conflicting signals. Many people, when they get a new dog, (particularly those with no experience in keeping dogs) tend to be over-indulgent and soft. They do not treat the dog as an animal, preferring to make it a member of their family. In other words they make the classic mistake of humanizing the dog, giving it a status within the household that it doesn't warrant or deserve.

In the chapter 'Understanding the Mind of Your Dog' I have described the wolf pack hierarchical system and how a young wolf learns the pecking order and where it fits into the social scale. I drew a direct line between the Alpha male and discipline of both the pack and the individual which is achieved by dominance.

A dog that starts to show aggression as it matures into a young adult is simply becoming dominant, he is challenging you, trying to establish his place in the pecking order. You and your family have become junior pack members and he is trying to show dominance. If this is allowed to continue then you have real problems. The simple answer to avoid this situation is to teach the young dog discipline during its puppyhood.

I never fail to be astonished at the attitudes of some people who bring problem dogs to me, many of them would rather smack their children than smack their dog. Yet when it is explained to them, they quickly see the sense in what I advocate. I believe that the foundation of all dog training – irrespective of what you eventually want the dog to do – is to train him the natural way his brain works. If you have given the dog a happy and secure upbringing and introduced him to discipline, if you have taught him that if you tell him to 'sit' you say 'sit' once. If he disobeys or ignores you do not raise your voice and shout the command again, you will simply compound the problem. People try to put authority into their voices by raising them, and if the dog gets used to it then he will continue to ignore you. So if your dog disobeys or ignores you, get a hold of him and very firmly push him down repeating the word 'sit' quietly .

If your young dog ever growls at you, no matter what the reason, – moving his bed, touching his feed bowl, grooming him – you must react instantly by punishing him by smacking him firmly. He must realize that the result of growling at you the 'Alpha' male or female gets him instant retribution.

As I have previously said it is totally unacceptable for any dog ever to bite a person. A young dog showing aggression can quickly be shown the folly of his ways if you react immediately. The questions I am often asked are, where should I hit him and how hard? The answer to the first question is ideally over his hindquarters, how hard to smack really is as long as a piece of string. Are we talking about some small skinny little Spaniel or a large Retriever with a thick coat? The answer is, use your common sense. If you're going to punish the dog by smacking him, the smack should be hard enough that he feels it, without, obviously causing damage. What is certain is that if you are too gentle it will not have the desired effect.

Some dog trainers who work with pets and domestic dogs subscribe to what is known as 'positive training'. This means that you 'reward the good and ignore the bad'. While some advocates of this form of training are no doubt genuine, and well-meaning, it has been my experience over many years and with many hundreds of problem dogs of all breeds from Jack Russells to Bull Mastiffs and even an Akita, that 'positive training' is a nonsense. It is a soft option that sounds nice and is politically correct but is fundamentally flawed because it attributes a degree of intelligence to the dog that it simply does not have and ignores the dog's pack instincts.

Dogs are simple creatures. Of course they have intelligence but we must not humanize them, attributing to them an ability to use their brain, to be able to somehow distinguish between a right and wrong, good and bad, that they simply are incapable of ever comprehending. It is simpler, quicker and less traumatic to the dog, he will learn much quicker if his foundation of discipline is taught in a natural way using his natural instincts.

From a very early age some puppies can be introduced to fairly sharp discipline, a good example of this is that some puppies can get quite aggressive while nursing and cause the bitch considerable discomfort. A bitch with an overtly aggressive pup will simply take it by the muzzle and bite the puppy firmly till it squeaks. After a few such bites it will feed more gently.

If you have built in to the foundation of your dog's training the knowledge that you will smack him, showing your disapproval if he misbehaves, then you will find that you avoid many of the problems that so many people encounter with their dogs. So that you are in no doubt, let me be absolutely clear, in my opinion a smack – when necessary – is an integral part of the early training of your dog. It is the quickest and most efficient way of establishing your relationship with your dog, the relationship of pack leader. He will have a greater respect for you, will want to be your friend, and will naturally look to you as leader.

If you do not establish your position as the unquestioned Alpha leader then you run the risk of confusing your dog. He will not respect you. You are essentially inviting him to do his own thing, to please himself, to disobey you and eventually he will naturally try and dominate.

## Electric collars

There is much confusion with most gundog owners on the subject of electric collars. Some people think they are cruel whilst others think that they are the panacea, the magical answer to training dogs. But are they necessary?

There is a considerable difference in the quality of dogs available in the UK and what is generally available in the US. In Britain there is an enormous gene pool of superb working blood lines. This arises for two reasons:

* The first is the prominence of field trials throughout the UK which has resulted in an

*A yellow Labrador fitted with an electric training collar.* (JAMES DOUGLAS)

abundance of quality puppies with proven working parents of the highest standard.
• The second reason is the number of rough shooters, as well as an abundance of driven shoots throughout the country. There is great emphasis put on quality dogs and you need only look through the 'dogs for sale' ads in the shooting press to find plenty of well-bred puppies.

These are puppies with all the natural instincts that will eventually make them into gundogs. They have a natural retrieving desire and drive. It would be ludicrous to consider using electrical stimuli when training these animals. Indeed you would be more likely to create problems where none previously existed.

Look how long we have had the two principal breeds in the UK. The Springer Spaniel has been around for many centuries and the Labrador Retriever for over two centuries. In that time they have been an integral part of British field sports.

Shooting is very different in the United States where it is much less controlled. Field trialling is also less popular. The average American gundog therefore has less quality in his breeding. It is for this reason that there is a constant demand in the United States for quality young dogs from Britain. However the cost of shipping these dogs makes them expensive, so it is normally the wealthier sportsmen who can afford them. The availability of proven high-quality puppies is more difficult to find in the US. They do exist, but there is also a plethora of puppies of less auspicious breeding. A good example of this was seen when I was filming at one of the top Pointer training kennels in the United States. They had dogs there which barely resembled the breeds they were meant to represent. Most of these dogs had very little natural working instincts, so the technique that they were compelled to employ was a combination of electric stimulus and force training.

## The anti-bark collar

There are two types of electric collar, the anti-bark collar, and the training collar first let us look at the anti- bark collar. A dog which is a habitual barker can be an absolute nightmare in a kennel. A habitual barker is a dog that barks non-stop and this can result in him stressing his cardiovascular system. The constant barking can also be a real nuisance to the dog's owner and his neighbours. If the dog is in a kennel block with other dogs the constant barking can result in setting the other dogs off and creating aggression in them, a situation which can be highly unsettling for both people and dogs within earshot.

If you realize that the principal reason a dog is likely to start barking is to draw attention to itself, to get you to come and pay attention to him, then going in beside him and chastizing him has little or no effect. A habitual barker almost puts itself into a trance. I have seen one dog bark so continuously that his throat was swollen and obviously painful. The dog was in distress yet still he continued to try to bark.

The anti-bark collar allows the trainer to administer a stimulus which very quickly stops the dog barking. The collar has a little computerized box with a voice sensor and two small electrical prongs. Built into the computer system is a maximum of nine shocks. The first three operate on fifty per cent of the barks, the second three on thirty per cent of the barks, and the third three on ten per cent of the barks. Then the system switches off.

When the dog barks, a buzzer in the box sounds on the collar under the dog's chin. Five seconds later a small shock is administered. The dog assumes that the bark caused the discomfort. When he barks again the buzzer rings, acting as a warning, When he barks again the buzzer rings again and five seconds later he gets a further small shock. It does not take the dog long to realize that his barking is causing the discomfort and the barking stops. I once had a particularly loud habitual barker in my kennel, a black Labrador dog by the name of Zonker. He had been driving his owners, and their neighbours, crazy. After a dose of the electric collar, Zonker barked three times then stopped!

The advantage of an anti-bark collar is that the dog's owner is not there so the dog cannot associate the discomfort with him. The use of the anti-bark collar, whilst not being to my liking, is a fairly simple choice. A habitual barker has no future, but by stopping his incessant barking he becomes a normal dog.

## The training collar

The training collar has now been developed into a sophisticated piece of equipment very different from the crude devices first introduced during the 1950s and originally developed to stop dogs chasing deer and livestock.

Trainers soon saw the potential of this equipment in some of the states of America where snakes are a problem. A rattlesnake with its fangs withdrawn is placed in brush. A young dog with a training collar fitted is worked towards where the snake is hidden. As soon as the dog shows it has winded the snake, the trainer administers a shock to the dog. It doesn't take the dog many lessons of this kind before it makes the connection between the smell of the snake and the shock. After that a dog that winds a snake rather than showing curiosity and going closer will back off fast!

The technique of training a Retriever with electrical stimulus is so detailed that it justifies a book on that subject alone, and it would be inappropriate in this book to enter into the detail of the use of the electric collar.

Whilst I do not use an electric training collar and do not advocate the use of them I have the advantage of working with dogs of excellent breeding with many natural qualities and instincts. Trainers in the United States however take a different view as they may be dealing with dogs with little natural quality. They also have the time factor to consider. As a general rule dog owners in the United States want their dogs trained quickly. A friend of mine – one of the premier retriever trainers in the US – explained to me that he treats all dogs the same, he collar-conditions them then puts them through his training regime. There are no exceptions, they are all trained with electric collar stimulation and force training.

It is also important that anyone ever considering using an electric collar should be properly trained in their use. In the right hands they can be an efficient and useful aid to training an obtuse dog. In the wrong hands, used incorrectly, they can do irreparable harm.

When I was filming *Water Dogs–Training Retrievers* for the American market, we used one of the top retriever training kennels in the US as a location. The dogs we showed working in the video had been trained with electrical stimuli and were quite superb and impressive. It convinced me that if the trainer is properly trained and uses the collar responsibly they can do the job most effectively and are a valuable training aid.

## Force training

When I first became aware of force training I thought it was some kind of sick joke. A well-known trainer from one of the southern states was visiting my kennels. When he was leaving he presented me with a signed copy of his latest book. It contained photographs illustrating how he force trained dogs, and I read it with incredulity.

Years later when I was visiting a training kennels in the United States, the technique was fully demonstrated to me. My initial distaste was tempered when I realized that it was the only way that the majority of these dogs would ever learn to retrieve. I asked the simple question, 'would it not be better to work with dogs with more quality and natural abilities?'

The answer from the senior trainer was simple. 'Of course it would but these are the dogs the customers bring here and we've got to train them one way or the other.'

What is force training? A long table or bench is built against the wall of a building with a running wire stretched above the head height of the dog. The animal is stood on the table with a chain from its collar attached to the running wire. If the dog tries to jump off the table the trainer restrains it. A cord is tied around the dog's wrist and looped round his two middle toes. With a pull on the cord the trainer can pinch the nerves of the toes causing pain. While he is pinching the toes, the trainer places a small dummy in the dog's mouth. The instant the dog holds the dummy the string (which is pinching the toes) is released and the pain stops.

This technique is continued until the dog has learned that it can switch off the pain by picking up the retrieve on command. It certainly works and after a few training sessions on the table even the most reluctant retriever is picking up.

Force training is also used for stopping a dog to either voice or whistle. Watching a demonstration of this particular technique I felt that it removed the dignity from the dog and made the trainer appear rather callous. In fact the trainer was a sensitive man. He was demonstrating the only training technique he had been taught and did not realize that there were other methods he could have used.

*In the United States some trainers use a captive running wire when introducing dogs to early retrieving.* (JAMES DOUGLAS)

An up-turned metal bin was placed on uneven ground below a wooden structure similar to a gallows with two tall posts with a cross bar at the top. Attached to the centre of the crossbar was a small pulley wheel. A skinny little reddish dog – vaguely resembling an Irish Setter – was placed on the metal bin with a rope running from his collar along his back, looped around his abdomen, up through the pulley wheel and down to the trainer's hand.

The dog could not jump off the metal bin as the trainer simply restrained him. The dog was obviously frightened and stood with all four feet on the bin as the trainer gently told the dog to 'whoa' while he explained to me how the system worked. The dog quickly learned that if it moved the bin would wobble, since the ground underneath was uneven and the dog felt insecure. The only way the dog could have a secure footing was to stand motionless. In this way the dog learned that on the command of 'whoa' it should stop and stand motionless.

A variation of this 'whoa' command was shown to me with a large German Wire-haired Pointer. A rope was passed from the dog's collar, along his back and round his abdomen – almost like a carrying handle. From the middle of the rope another rope was passed up and over the bough of an oak tree. The trainer held the other end of the rope and on the command of 'whoa' hoisted the animal several inches off the ground.

Immediately the animal's feet started to leave the ground he felt insecure and naturally gripped with all four feet standing motionless. If he tried to move he was immediately hoisted back into the air. The dog quickly learned that on the command of 'whoa' he should stand still.

It is undeniable that these force-training techniques work. In my opinion, however, they are distasteful and unpleasant, compelling the dog to obey through fear. For me the whole integrity and essence of training a dog is that every effort should be made to make it a pleasurable experience for both the trainer and the pupil so that he becomes a willing companion who enjoys being with you rather than a servile one.

# 11
# FIELD TRIALS

Field trials and working tests are an important aspect of the gundog scene, and it is through the ever-changing world of trialling dogs that we keep the high standard of work and abilities in the best of our dogs. Gundog owners fall into two categories – the shooting man who has a working dog as a necessary extension to his sport, and the dog man who shoots – the latter is prepared to put much more work into his gundog and gets a great deal of pleasure from training and working him. It is the man more orientated to dog work who is likely to enjoy trialling, which can be a very rewarding experience. Most gundogs, however, never see a trial, their owners being content to have the dog purely for their own interest and sport, being uninterested in any form of competition. This is unfortunate, since a healthy competitive spirit can only improve the gundog trainer's appreciation of his dog, and has the distinct advantage of encouraging the trainer to strive for higher standards.

If you want to try competing, then it is as well to prepare yourself and your dog. You should remember that the field trialling world, like any other community, has its personalities, its likes and dislikes, and it is a fact of life that your face must fit. Therefore you should always approach any group of trialling enthusiasts as very much the new boy, and whatever you do, do not assume that you are going to set the heather alight, or win straight away, irrespective of how good you think your dog is. Most experienced trialling men and women, however, are only too pleased to see new faces, and are willing to give help and advice, if asked.

This chapter is intended to give you a general guide to what to expect at field trials, but no book can substitute for the experience of going to several trials as a spectator and experiencing the day. Do not be afraid to ask what the form is, and you will find that after a few enjoyable days as a spectator you will be better prepared to take your dog into the arena. It is better to do this than stay away and try to do all your preparation from books.

If you think you are going to try trialling you should approach the field trial society relevant to your breed of dog as soon as possible. You must have registered your dog with the Kennel Club (which you should do have done anyway). Start going to trials before your dog is old enough to enter, and you will see the standard your dog will have to achieve if he is to have any chance of success.

The work required of dogs in a trial is really only a refined, polished and compacted version of what is expected of a dog in the shooting field. So do not be put off or intimidated and think you may not be good enough. Just prepare your dog and work on his training, using everything you have observed at the different events you visit. If you have joined a field trials society, visited trials and let it be known that you intend to enter your dog, you will have a better chance of your dog being accepted for a place. Often, more dogs are entered than can possibly be accommodated in the time allotted and so, as a general rule, new members have to wait until the more established ones are drawn.

*A Labrador competing in a gundog working test at the Scottish Game Fair.* (David Hudson)

## Getting the dog ready

You will be expected to work your dog, giving a minimum of commands, so it is better if you spend considerable time sharpening up his communication with you. Treat him like an athlete. It is virtually impossible to keep any animal at peak condition all the time, so in the weeks prior to an event, put greater emphasis on his physical fitness as well as his work. If you are starting to give your dog additional exercise by working him hard, then it is necessary to step up his protein intake so that you achieve peak condition, both mentally and physically, in time for the event.

Nothing tires a dog more than a long car journey before being expected to perform. So make a decision. If the event you are entering is far enough away to justify an overnight stay, then this would be a wise decision. Then on the morning of the event, both you and the dog will be bright and alert and much more prepared for the day's activity. In many ways it is a case of psyching yourself up. If you decide to drive on the same day, make sure you get there in plenty of time.

On the morning of the trial, give your dog a light, high-protein breakfast, and a restricted exercise period of no more than fifteen to twenty minutes. It is too late to start adding any last minute lessons. You have committed yourself and it is better to concentrate on relaxing both you and your dog. Try not to take it too seriously, luck has as much to do with winning as in any other competitive activity. Most important, try to avoid tension or nerves. Your dog will quickly pick up on your state of mind and neither of you will give of your best.

When you arrive at the trial location, keep your dog on the lead. You should be seen to be doing the right thing. Find the secretary or organizer of the day, introduce yourself and inform him or her of the number you have been allotted. Unless you are one of the first dogs to run, go and join the other competitors in the audience and enjoy the event.

## Field tests

An excellent guide to the sort of competition, control and experience of the test and trial business is for your to enter your dog in several field tests before you consider higher things. A field test is very simple, and is purely a test of the basic requirements of any working dog. You will be expected to do no more than you would in any training exercise. Dogs are given a series of simple retrieves – always with dummies – and with no unmarked retrieves. The advantage of the field test is that the dog performs on his own, without the additional distraction of another working with him.

There are many field tests run throughout the country and they do not involve as much officialdom and formality as trials. You do not, for instance, have to be a member of the society, since most field tests are run by gun clubs and local field sports organizations.

The natural progression from the field test is the novice trial, and although you will be expected to work with live game, novice trials do not have anything like the pressure, tension and feelings of high competition in an open trial. During a novice trial there is a more relaxed atmosphere and the judges are much less demanding and more forgiving. It is after all a trial for young and less experienced dogs.

It is through the natural progression of tests and novice trials that you and your dog become refined, tuned, and prepared for the much more demanding work of the trial.

## Spaniel trials

In Spaniel trials two dogs work simultaneously, with two judges each judging one dog apiece. As your turn in the trial approaches, the steward will indicate to you that you should come to the front. Whatever you do, do not leap forward, pre-guessing the judge's requirements. Remain behind him until he asks you to take your place in the line. At that time you should take the lead from your dog, take your place and the trial will begin.

The dogs will be asked to hunt vigorously for the two guns who walk on either side of you. Be diligent in making sure that your dog works his ground efficiently and goes right to the outside edges of his allotted avenue or area. Watch carefully. The instant the dog flushes, peep the stop whistle. If the game is shot, wait until the judge indicates whether he would prefer your dog to retrieve the game or not. Do not assume he will expect a retrieve. Wait until he asks you.

While your dog is working, if you hear a shot being fired from the other end of the line – over the other dog – drop your dog immediately using your whistle. Here a slightly different question may arise. The other judge may decide he does not want his dog to retrieve, and if you have not yet had an opportunity to give your dog a retrieve, your judge may well ask you if you would like

*Competitors waiting for their turn to run at a Cocker Spaniel field trial.* (DAVID HUDSON)

to take it. While it is not obligatory that you take a retrieve shot down the line, it is good manners to do so. However, do not send your dog out before you have ascertained exactly where the retrieve lies. The sense of this is quite obvious. There is little point in trying to work your dog on a blind retrieve when you have only a vague notion of its location.

Do not get frustrated or angry. Never resort to shouting and try at all times to act the very model of the perfect dog handler, even if your dog is misbehaving outrageously.

Eventually the judge will feel that he has adequately assessed your dog, and will indicate that – for the moment at least – he is finished with you. Put your dog on the lead and drop back amongst the followers. Whether your dog has behaved brilliantly, or done everything wrong, stay calm.

You will be called forward again, this time to work for the second judge. The time between your first and second run can vary. If there have been a number of eliminations, you may well be called on pretty soon, so don't vanish off back to your car for a cup of coffee. Stay on hand, show interest in the proceedings, and be there so that when you are called you can step forward immediately. Your second run should be similar to the first.

If you discover that luck has not been with you that day and you have been eliminated, accept the judges' decision with good grace. Equally, if you find that you are amongst the winners, accept the situation gracefully. In your next trial you may well discover you fail miserably.

Remember that in the excitement of the day things may well go wrong, and no matter how frustrating it is when your dog commits some misdemeanour you know is certainly not typical, it is his actions on that particular day that the judges look at. They are not only looking for style, general work and response to handling, but also the dog's ability to carry out the work expected of the breed. You will be disqualified if the dog chases game, fails on a retrieve, damages game, barks, whines or generally gives tongue, runs over ground missing game, lifts and retrieves unshot game, and does not give up the retrieve on command. You will also be disqualified if the dog runs in, either to the fall of game or shot.

When all the dogs have run and the trial has finished, the judges will confer. If they are not in agreement as to the winning dogs, they will normally ask for a run-off. This would normally involve three or four dogs, who would be expected to run at the same time, giving the judges a better opportunity to watch them working at the same time. From this run-off the judges would make a decision. Finally certificates are presented and general congratulations handed out.

Whether you are amongst the winners or not, you and your dog will have learned much from the experience, so that when you return to your next trial, you will both be better prepared for whatever you are asked to do.

## Retriever trials

The type of work and performances required at Retriever trials differs in many ways from a Spaniel trial. The main difference is, of course, that a Retriever is not expected to hunt game. The judges will be expecting – and should get – a very high standard of control and expertise in the dogs' retrieving work.

When not called on to work, your Retriever will be expected to stay happily and confidently at heel, and act like a gentleman. The work required of a Retriever in a trial is slightly different from what is expected of their dogs by the majority of Retriever owners, and in this slight difference the two types of dog are worlds apart.

The average rough shooting Retriever owner prefers his dog to hunt in front of him. Certainly he will not do it as effectively as a Spaniel or HPR, but unless your shooting is exclusively driven (i.e. standing at a peg) almost all Retriever owners will have encouraged their dogs to hunt and flush, and drop to flush, albeit at a fairly close range.

Trialling dogs are not expected to hunt in any way, but to be able to carry out a long, difficult retrieve, where there is great emphasis placed on the handler's ability to work the dog out on these distant retrieves, to the exclusion of all other distractions, either fur or feathered, that might be in the dog's path. If a Retriever's natural instinct to hunt has been developed and refined, if he has been trained to work that bit closer to the handler, then he will be less prepared to work on very long, blind retrieves.

Therefore the preparation of a Retriever for a trial will involve greater emphasis on your hand signals, and you would do well to dwell diligently on the chapter in this book describing the use of walls and fences to give your dog experience on long straight runs on command, whether it is left, right, or straight back. Once a Retriever has experienced that when you wave him in a particular direction – even for a few hundred metres – he will be rewarded by finding a retrieve, then he will have greater confidence in following your signal. It is only a distance barrier that you have to break. When he understands that lining him up, setting him on a course and sending him away – followed by the peep of your whistle and the 'steady' command – will result in him making a find, then the distance work should present few problems.

As with other trials, Retriever trials are in front of an audience, with other dogs working too. It is important, therefore, that you pay attention to your dog's confidence when others are about and make sure he learns to ignore other dogs. To teach him this, take him to the local clay pigeon club. Keep him on the lead and stand well back when you first introduce him to this new sound of people, noise and shouting. Progressively move closer, until you are standing behind one of the busiest stands, with the dog sitting at your heel, watching the proceedings. Discourage anyone from making a fuss of your dog by simply telling them that you are there to give your dog experience of ignoring others.

When you enter a trial, there is a little trick you can employ. The majority of participants and the audience at trials are dressed in drab green – Barbour coats, caps and green wellies. From a distance they can all look the same to a dog. So give your dog a little help. Wear something distinctive – a lighter coloured coat, a yellow scarf or an equally noticeable garment. Of course, you would have to wear the same garment whenever you train the dog. One eminent trainer I know wears a garish tartan cap when he trials. It may be a small help, but it is certainly worth considering.

The judges will be assessing the dog's style, marking capabilities, ability to take directions and retrieve beautifully to hand – and all this carried out with a minimum of noise. They will also be looking for speed, style, and the general set of the dog, his carriage and his flair. He will be eliminated if he barks or gives tongue, if he damages game, is hard mouthed, if he runs in, refuses to enter or cross water, or goes out of control. He will also be eliminated if he changes birds. While it is not allowed for a dog to drop a bird during a retrieve, it is acceptable if, after his initial collection, he lays the bird down to get a better grip and balance on the retrieve.

Never try to hoodwink the judge. If, for instance, your dog brings you a bird which you think may be damaged, do not try turning your back on the judge as you take the retrieve as you try to smooth down the feathers. Most judges have seen just about every trick in the book and are fully aware that birds can be damaged during a fall, particularly if it has hit stony or frozen ground.

A Retriever trial would normally involve three or four judges walking in line. In the case of three judges, each would judge two dogs working in front of him, with six dogs working at the same time. In the case of four judges, they would normally work in pairs, with only four dogs working at the same time.

Once you have been called into the line, take your place, and as the line moves forward, game will be put up and shot. The judges will indicate which dog they wish to take the retrieve. Do not assume that if a bird falls in front of you, you will be asked to retrieve it. The judges have the overall picture to consider and may well decide that retrieves should be taken by dogs further up or down the line.

Throughout the procedure your dog should be sitting quietly at your side, giving no sign of anxiety. He should not fidget or make a sound, but should watch the other dogs working in front of him. If you are asked to take an unmarked retrieve from further down the line, you must pay attention to the wind direction before you send your dog out, and direct him downwind of where you know the game to be, before working him on to the retrieve. When the judge is satisfied that he has seen enough from your dog he will tell you, and you can rejoin the audience. During your second run, although you will be under a different judge, the procedure will be the same. If you are at a trial which involves a drive, your dog will be expected to behave as he would or should during any formal day's shooting. He must sit patiently and quietly, observing the shooting going on around him, and must not be tempted to move as the birds fall around him. Even if a runner passes close to him he must make no attempt to move after it.

## HPR trials

As the various breeds of HPR dogs have become popular so too have the trials and tests, and it has become an increasingly competitive field. An HPR trial is little different to what would be expected of the dog on a normal well-run shooting day. The dogs are run individually under two judges, and the dog is expected to work in front of two or three guns walking in line.

When you are called forward to take your place, go forward to the judge, take the lead off the dog and cast it out. The HPR is expected to quarter the line well, so make sure he goes right to the far edges of his space. As he turns and quarters the ground, he should do so with flair and confidence, coming on a rock-steady point, and holding it until the gun is in position and ready to shoot. The dog should then flush on command, and remain exactly where it is until told to retrieve. If, after the game has been flushed, it flies off unscathed, the dog must resume his quartering on command.

Because of the diverse abilities of the HPRs, they can be more interesting to watch, since the trial will involve different types of terrain which test the dogs as fully as possible in each type of environment. The dog would be expected to work through light woodland and either over open arable land or moorland, and would be asked to do at least one water retrieve.

## Pointer and Setter trials

Trials for Pointers and Setters are a little different from the other trial disciplines in that they mostly take place during the close season and no game is shot. Pointers and Setters are not required to retrieve during their trials so stakes are run during July and August in the weeks immediately before grouse shooting starts, or in the spring and in early September. The spring trials take place in Scotland on grouse and in East Anglia on paired partridges in young corn. The summer trial circuit is all on grouse moors, starting in mid-July in England and gradually working northwards to end in the north of Scotland on the eve of the Twelfth, and then the triallers meet up again in the east of England for the autumn stakes run on partridges and pheasants among the stubble fields.

Spaniel, Retriever and HPR trials take place at intervals throughout the shooting season and competitors might run their dogs once a week or once a fortnight, depending on how often they enter and what luck they have in the draw for places. At the Pointer and Setter trials it is quite possible for a dog to run in three or four stakes in a single week and perhaps ten or a dozen stakes in a month during the summer trials in July and August. Your dog needs to be very fit to stand up to this sort of schedule, though you can of course enter only one or two trials if time does not allow you to do the whole circuit.

There are stakes for puppies, novice dogs and, for those dogs that have qualified by being placed in a puppy or novice stake, open and all-aged events, plus breed stakes that are limited to entrants from a particular breed. The format is the same for all stakes. A draw is made for the running order and the dogs are always run in a brace: that is, two dogs are run at the same time. Two judges assess the work of each brace and may decide to call both, either or neither of the dogs to run in subsequent rounds.

*Handlers with an Irish Setter and a Pointer ready for their turn at the Pointer and Setter Champion Stake.* (DAVID HUDSON)

The dogs have to quarter the beat allocated to them by the judges, find any game on that beat and point it. Once on point they must remain steady until the judge asks the handler to send the dog in to flush the birds. A shot will be fired into the air as the birds go away and the dog should sit or drop to flush or shot. Certain faults such as flushing game, chasing fur or feather, running out of control or giving tongue will eliminate a dog automatically. Provided that the dog has not committed one of these eliminating faults he may be brought back for a second run in front of the judges.

I say 'may be brought back' because it is not enough simply to avoid making any major errors. Pointer and Setter judges are also looking at a very high overall standard of work from the dogs they are judging. In order to win a trial a dog has to show excellent pace when quartering, point firmly and positively, rode in confidently to produce its birds and back its brace mate if the other dog has a find. Dogs that commit any serious fault, or that fail to exhibit the sort of quality that the judges are seeking are often discarded very quickly in order that the better dogs have a longer opportunity to show their paces. With up to forty dogs to be judged in a single day the judges simply don't have time to waste on dogs that don't come up to scratch.

After two, three or sometimes even four rounds, the judges will decide on the winner and the minor places, provided of course that any dog has impressed them sufficiently to merit an award. With the very high standards that are expected of the runners in Pointer and Setter trials it is not unusual for the top honours to be withheld or even for no awards at all to be made, so if you are among the prizes you can be assured that you and your dog have done well. Even for those that do not win, the friendly atmosphere at the trials coupled with the often magnificent surroundings can more than make up for any disappointment.

## Spring pointing tests

Spring pointing tests for the Hunt, Point and Retrieve breeds are held in March and April each year. These are not field trials: the dogs are not competing against one another but are measured by the judges against a standard and graded accordingly.

Dogs below two years old are graded on partridge or pheasant, but those over two years are graded only by their handling of partridge, pheasants and other game being used only to assess the dogs' steadiness. The tests are designed to examine a dog's natural hunting ability including ground treatment, game finding, staunchness on point, pace and steadiness when game is produced. The dogs run singly, into the wind, and are expected to quarter a good, wide beat with pace and style and to find and point all game birds on the beat and to run for at least ten minutes in order to qualify for grading.

The judges can rate the dogs in three categories: excellent, very good or good, with any dog not reaching the required standard for a 'good' rating remaining unclassified. One particularly helpful feature of the spring pointing tests, especially for the beginner to trials and tests, is the verbal critique that the judges give at the end of the day when they say what they thought of each runner – and handler. The spring pointing tests are an excellent precursor to the more serious business of field trials as well as providing some interest at a time of the year that is usually quiet as far as dog work is concerned.

*HPRs like this Hungarian Vizsla can compete in spring pointing tests on paired partridges as well as regular field trials.* (DAVID HUDSON)

\* \* \* \* \* \*

Luck plays an enormous part in trials but it is an interesting and exciting extension of your dog's work, and perseverance and hard work will bring great results.

# 12

# BREEDING

Everyone who owns a bitch will at some point ask themselves whether they want to breed from her. Is it beneficial to have puppies? The answer is simple; the benefits of having them can be outweighed by the problems that may be caused by the pregnancy and birth. In other words, the one can cancel out the other.

It seems that bitches who have had a litter are less prone to trouble with their reproductive system in later years, but there can also be adverse effects caused by having a litter. However, bitches do come into season – usually twice a year – and it is just bad luck if she manages to time this in the middle of the shooting season. Some bitches can be worked for the first week of their season, as long as they are working on their own, or in the company of other bitches. But if there is a dog about, the whole exercise becomes rather silly, since even the best trained dogs quickly forget their training once they get wind of the compelling scent of a bitch in season. So if you have a bitch that has come into heat during the shooting season, leave her at home.

There are tablets and sprays available from the chemist or your vet. However, they are not the cure-all, acting more as a dissuader to dogs hanging around your door, and would certainly not provide protection you could rely on during a day's shooting. Also, some bitches when they come into season, seem to lose all semblance of sense and want to do nothing more than remain by their owner's side, or worse – particularly if a bitch has been served before. In that instance there is a greater compunction for her to follow her natural instincts. One GSP bitch I trained was a great dog and 100 per cent reliable as a good, solid, working dog. Yet when she came into season she lost all control of her senses. She was not only unwilling to work, but seemed unhappy if she got any further than a few yards from my side. She was not even prepared to sit in a car if I left her for a short time, but would make every effort to get out of the vehicle in her desire to stay with me.

## A bitch's season

You should normally get some warning that your bitch is coming into season. Her vulva will swell quite noticeably and small drops of blood and fluid will appear. Some bitches are quite scrupulous in their efforts to keep themselves clean, licking and washing themselves constantly, while others are less interested and can become quite soiled. A season lasts, on average, twenty-one days, and if you are intending to have puppies then you must watch your bitch carefully.

About ten days after the beginning of her season the fluid discharge will change colour and become clearer. If you are going to have the bitch served, it is between the tenth and thirteenth day that conception is most likely to take place. The fluid will continue to seep until the end of her season. If, during her season, there is the slightest possibility that she may have been caught by a dog, and you want to avoid the chance of an unwanted pregnancy, take her immediately to the vet who will give her an injection to terminate the pregnancy.

## Should you have your bitch mated?

Everyone who owns a gundog has a responsibility to behave correctly and to try at all times to maintain a high standard of dog stock. You must be honest with yourself and not fall to the temptation of having a litter for either financial or emotional reasons. If your dog is a poor specimen, if she suffers from an hereditary defect, such as being under- or over-shot, you have a duty not to have puppies from her, otherwise you are perpetuating the very problems that so many people interested in gundogs work hard to eradicate.

## False pregnancy

If you are not familiar with the condition of false pregnancy, it can be quite alarming, and an understanding of what is happening to your bitch will help you to know how to react. False pregnancy is not an uncommon occurrence, and can take the form of a simple swelling of the abdomen, usually six to nine weeks after she has been in season. This swelling may last a few days and recede, but in some dogs it can continue to grow, almost as though the dog was genuinely pregnant, until eventually the animal becomes quite broody, and may even start to prepare a nest, as though a litter of pups was imminent. A bitch in this condition will often take possession of some piece of familiar household equipment – it can be a child's doll, or even an old slipper – and she will direct all her maternal instincts towards it and appear to treat it exactly as she would a puppy, carrying it about and being very possessive.

If your bitch starts to develop false pregnancy symptoms, take her straight to the vet who should prescribe a course of tablets. Whatever you do, do not let the condition take its course. You can cause the bitch considerable suffering, confusion and mental anguish. You can greatly help a bitch that has this condition if you make sure she has plenty of exercise, is not allowed unlimited liquid and is kept away from heat.

## Spaying

Spaying is another subject that suffers a great deal from lack of knowledge, and although it may be unnecessary to include the subject in a book on gundogs, I feel it is relevant to discuss the subject, to avoid misunderstandings.

Though the operation is a relatively simple exercise for any vet, and has the advantage that the bitch will no longer come into season, or be susceptible to uterine problems in her later years, it is not, in my opinion, a course of action that I would advise. If you choose a bitch you should accept the responsibility of the animal and its gender, rather than try to avoid the minor inconveniences by resorting to surgery.

Some people claim that they prefer the more mellow temperament which can be induced by spaying. But to me this is an excuse, reflecting the owner's inability to cope with the dog. It is a widely held belief that after spaying, bitches become fat and lethargic. This is not true. A spayed bitch has, in general, a more mellow temperament, and consequently requires less food. Just like humans, the only way a dog will become fat and lethargic is by eating more food than the exercise it takes justifies.

## Castration

There is no reason that can justify having a dog castrated – other than severe aggressiveness or if the dog habitually runs away, straying in search of pastures new. Although in some cases castration may cure these problems it should rarely be considered. Rather than resorting to surgery to try and improve an undesirable dog, it is preferable to start again with a better and more desirable puppy.

## Mating

At its simplest, breeding of dogs can be left to a bitch in season and the nearest dog. They will get on with it, without any assistance, and in due course pups will probably appear. However, if you are seriously interested in either allowing your dog to be used to serve a bitch, or having puppies from your bitch, then you must consider several things. If you possess a dog, and someone asks you to oblige them with a service, you should ask yourself if your dog is an excellent specimen, or does he possess any faults which are undesirable. Having satisfied yourself that your dog is suitable, then you must appraise the bitch and ask the same questions about her. There is little point in perpetuating undesirable physical or character faults. It is too easy to be greedy and everyone who is interested in gundogs has a responsibility to make every effort to do their part to keep dogs as near to the standard of the breed as possible.

If the dogs are suitable, examine their pedigrees and make sure that they do not have too many common recent ancestors. If you are in any doubt as to their suitability, then any competent dog breeder could easily advise you.

If you have a good quality bitch and rather than just using any handy dog of the same breed, book a service with a top quality Field Trials Champion. In this way you take a great deal of the guesswork out of the union, and of course, have a much greater chance of getting a better price for the puppies and passing on a much better quality puppy.

*A beautiful yellow Labrador. It is essential to breed only from the best specimens if the the high standard of our gundogs is to be maintained.* (TERRY SCROGGIE)

The use of a dog from a professional kennel has many things to recommend it. First of all, if you are inexperienced in the actual mating process, it will not matter, since the dog's owner will handle the whole affair. Book your dog's service well in advance, since the owner of the stud dog will certainly have to satisfy himself that your bitch is suitable and also slot her into the calendar so he doesn't have too many bitches arriving at the same time.

The standard practice with professionals is to charge a flat fee. This is preferable to the sort of arrangement which often takes place between two friends, where the dog owner will normally have the pick of the litter. This works well only if your bitch has several puppies. However, I have known of cases where a bitch has had one or two pups. The owner of the dog takes his, as arranged, leaving the owner of the bitch having done all the work and ending up with one, or even no pups. So it is preferable that you agree a fee with the owner of the dog and make sure that whatever arrangements you come to, everything is agreed before the service takes place.

It is ill advised to consider taking a litter of puppies form your bitch before she is an adult and her training is complete, and certainly not before her second birthday. Try to time the mating so that the puppies will be born during the spring or early summer months. This makes everything so much easier. The temperature is warmer and it gives the pups a better start than having to cope with the cold and wet, as they would if they were born later in the year.

Watch for your bitch coming into season. From the first signs that her season has started you have ten to twelve days to wait before she will reach the stage where conception is likely. Watch the colour of the fluid discharge from her vulva and when it starts to change, this is the best time to introduce her to the dog. You should give the dog owner advance warning of the start of the bitch's season so he will know to within a day when you are best to introduce the two dogs.

When you do this they may immediately get down to business, or the bitch may skip about for a little while before standing for the dog, with her tail to one side. If she is not prepared to stand, then you may be a day too early, although in the case of maiden bitches if you are absolutely certain of your dates it may be necessary for you to hold her firmly to allow the dog to mount. This course of action should, however, only be used as a last resort.

The best way to go about it, unless the dogs are immediately enthusiastic, is to put them in a quiet run where they will not be disturbed, and retire out of sight, where you can keep your eye on them discreetly. After the dog has mounted the bitch he may tie, though this is not always the case. After the dog has served the bitch, if he has tied, go into the run and hold the bitch's head, soothing her, while the owner of the dog does the same.

At this point the dogs should normally be standing tail to tail, with the dog's penis passing between his hind legs and into the bitch. Do not, under any circumstances, attempt to prise them apart or allow the bitch to pull. Keep the dogs together and quiet, and remain with them, holding their heads, until finally the dog comes free of his own accord.

At this point, if you have not witnessed this before, you may get a bit of a surprise. The dog's penis may appear as though something has gone wrong; the large, red, swollen, semi-erect appendage appearing unable to retract. This is entirely natural and no attempt should be made to assist the dog. If the conditions continues then seek medical advice, but this is most unlikely.

The chances of conception are enhanced if another service is arranged for the following day.

If you are using a young and inexperienced dog for the service, he may, in his enthusiasm, continually try to mount the bitch without actually penetrating. In this case you should take his penis and guide it into the vulva. Otherwise the dog may ejaculate uselessly before entering the bitch.

# The pregnancy

At first there may be no apparent sign of your bitch having conceived, though during the first three weeks the embryos will have fully developed. It is over the next six weeks that the puppies start to grow in the uterus, and you will see the bitch starting to show physical signs that she is in pup. Her nipples and udders will start to swell. It is important to prepare your bitch and pay attention to her condition during pregnancy. From conception, which you should mark in your calendar, the puppies will be carried for sixty-three days, although they can be born two or three days either side of the sixty-third.

Since she will carry the puppies for nine weeks, it is important that you increase her food for the first four-and-a-half weeks, then during the second term of four-and-a-half weeks, step up her food yet again. Do not simply resort to giving her an extra scoopful of food at normal evening meal times. Like you, she should not have just one enormous meal. It is better to start feeding her a meal in the morning in addition to the evening meal. In the second half of her pregnancy you can include a midday snack.

The motto for all puppies is that what you put into their formative months is what you will get out later in life. This means in bones and muscles, which start to develop before the puppies are born.

The growing puppies are going to make enormous demands on the bitch's system, drawing all the necessary nutrients they need to develop. Step up the quality of the food you give her, and pay attention to her protein intake and this is best done by making sure she has plenty of meat and fish. In addition, take the advice of your vet who will supply mineral supplements, which will provide her with all the trace elements that she needs. Of equal importance to her food is her exercise. You must prevent her from becoming fat and sluggish. If you allow her to become lazy, and do not ensure she has plenty of exercise, then she is more likely to have difficulties in the later stages of pregnancy.

At this time she will start to slow down, and it would be silly to expect her to still rush about as she may have done previously. You can still exercise her, but let her pace herself. Watch her general condition. If her back starts to really broaden, you may be over-feeding her, but don't cut down on her food drastically, instead feed her slightly less as you watch her condition.

Carefully plan for the time you expect your bitch to give birth. If she is kept in a kennel, make sure it is absolutely draught free, warm and dry. If possible fit an infra-red lamp, suspending it not less than a metre above the nest. If your bitch is in the house, prepare carefully for the event. A stout wooden box is ideal – the deeper the better, since high sides are desirable to prevent the puppies waddling out and it will also give the bitch a feeling of security. At this stage give her soft bedding. Collect plenty of newspaper to use during the birth and after the pups are born.

Try to encourage the bitch to use the box as a bed, which you should have placed in a quiet darkened area. Most bitches will show signs that the birth of the puppies is imminent. In the last few days before their arrival, she will become much more broody and will constantly scratch up her bedding in an attempt to make it more comfortable. Then about twenty-four hours before the pups are due, she will normally go off her food. When whelping actually begins, put newspapers under your bitch as bedding. Make sure you know how to contact your vet, in case anything goes wrong.

You will see the bitch's stomach starting to contract as she alternates pushing and straining to give birth, punctuated by periods of rest. When the pups start to appear, do not interfere. Keep yourself and the family quiet, and allow the bitch to do what she is competent at doing. As each puppy is born, she will eat the placenta, and lick the puppy until it is clean and dry. The placenta is nutritious, but if your bitch has more than five pups do not let her eat any more as they may cause diarrhoea.

The advantage of putting newspapers under the bitch will be seen as each puppy is born. Blood and fluid will be passed as each one comes out. The newspapers can be gently removed after each puppy is born so each subsequent one arrives on clean, dry paper.

The timing of the puppies' arrival can range from every half-hour to two hours, so do not be alarmed at any delay. As each pup is born it will be encased in a thin membrane which the bitch will wash off and eat. This is the only area where you may be called on to assist the bitch. When she is freeing the membrane, if she does not manage to get if from around the puppy's head, then you may gently peel it off. Apart from this, try not to interfere unless it is obvious something is going wrong.

If the puppies are born very quickly the bitch may not have sufficient time to get each puppy clean and dry. You can assist her by taking a clean, dry, soft towel and very gently drying any puppies she may have overlooked. If the umbilical cord is still attached, nip it with your fingernails (rather than cutting it with scissors). If you have to do this, however, take extreme care you do not put any pressure on the cord, or you may damage the puppy's stomach muscles.

In most cases, puppies are born without undue drama. Watch your bitch carefully, however. If she is still contracting and giving signs that she is still trying to push out another puppy after a period of about two-and-a-half hours then it is time to see your vet. Lastly, if, during the delivery of the pups, there is a foul smelling discharge, bile-like in consistency and green in colour, get your vet immediately.

Finally, a word of comfort. Having puppies may be a big event in your home, but it is only natural for the bitch, and she is capable of carrying off the whole process without your interference. You are there to gently soothe and comfort her and – if absolutely necessary – to lend a hand.

## The new puppies

The new puppies will need nothing that cannot be provided by the bitch. She will provide them with food, warmth and security in the first few weeks. You need only keep their bedding clean, and make sure the environment in which they are kept is warm, dry and draught free. It is the bitch you must pay attention to, making sure that you keep her on a high quality protein diet of fish, meat and a milk substitute which you get from your vet. Use the same feeding as you did before she had whelped, feeding her two or three times a day.

After about three weeks you should start to feed the puppies supplementary food of two small meals a day, consisting of milk and light cereals. It is not a good idea to give young puppies cows' milk but you can buy a milk-substitute specially formulated for puppies and whelping bitches from your vet.

Puppies must be taught to lap. Gently take a puppy and dip its mouth into a dish of lukewarm milk. This compels them to lick their muzzles and, having discovered the pleasant taste, they will soon start to lap. You can also encourage them to use their tongues by dipping your finger in the milk and allowing them to lick it off.

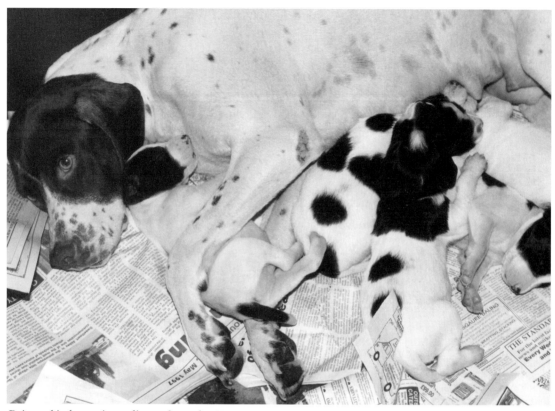

*Pointer bitch nursing a litter of puppies.* (DAVID HUDSON)

Gradually, between the ages of three and six weeks, increase the number of meals you feed your puppies, until they are having four meals a day. When they are five weeks old you can start adding a little meat – preferably cooked – but make sure that there is little or no fat included. You can also give them lightly boiled fish, but remove all the bones.

Feed the puppies a little and often. If you try to feed either your bitch or her puppies on the cheap, you will not get the best results. As the puppies are weaned on to solid meals, the bitch's milk will start to dry up so that by the age of six to seven weeks the puppies should be completely weaned from their mother. At this stage, discourage any puppies that persist in trying to suckle her, and once the suckling ceases the bitch's lactation will stop.

*The same Pointer working grouse a few months later.* (DAVID HUDSON)

Once your bitch is free from feeding the pups you can start a gentle fitness campaign, slowly building up the amount of exercise you give her. The exercise, combined with the natural elasticity of her muscles will start to tighten her tummy, and she should, with a little help from you, regain her former shape and condition fairly quickly.

## Worming

You will need to worm your puppies when they are four weeks old. All puppies are born with worms and you must ensure they are treated. Ask your vet for the appropriate treatments.

## Selling the puppies

If you have a good gundog, and have gone to the trouble of having the puppies sired by a top class dog, you may find that your puppies are sold before they are born. Certainly by passing the word amongst your shooting friends and acquaintances you can often find people who want to buy a quality puppy. However I do not advise that you let the puppies leave the nest before they are eight weeks old. Personally I prefer to keep my puppies till they are ten weeks. They develop so quickly and those extra two weeks can make a considerable difference as they mature mentally.

The reason I prefer to keep my puppies a bit longer is that it is fairly traumatic for them to suddenly find themselves on their own all way from their brothers and sisters and those extra two weeks make a difference, and therefore they are a lot less likely to develop behavioural problems in future years.

If you have not been fortunate enough to have had advance orders for your puppies amongst your friends then you should take an advertisement in the shooting/country press several weeks before you intend to let the puppies go.

Your responsibility does not end merely with selling the puppies. You have a duty to try to ensure that each one is going to a good, knowledgeable shooting home, or at least to the sort of home where you think the dog will be well cared for. Take a note of who has bought each puppy as it is often useful to keep in touch with the progress of the pups. Most important, try to spread the sale of the puppies over several days and preferably a couple of weeks. If all the puppies disappear too quickly it can be very traumatic for the bitch, causing her unnecessary distress and confusion.

Ensure that you get sufficient pedigree forms well in advance (from pet shops or vets) and write one out for each puppy before handing it over to the puppy's new owner. You can buy three or five generation pedigrees from the Kennel Club, which will come already printed with your dog's details, including the details of the owners of both sire and dam.

# 13
# THE YEARS TO COME

While the period of intense training which covers the first two years of your dog's life will eventually come to an end, and while you can relax and regard your dog as trained, you cannot afford to assume that all your hard work will last forever. Your dog will never forget all his training, but he can slide back and become slack and sloppy if you do not keep working at giving him regular training refreshers. Try to get into the habit, when you take him for a walk, of giving him the commands and having the same attitude to him as you would if you were on a training exercise. Never allow your dog to run free, for throughout his life you must remember that, no matter how well trained he is, if he is running free and out of your control, then he is doing his own thing and this will encourage him to slacken.

Many people ask the question: can a gundog be a housedog and a family pet? Of course he can. As he gains experience and mellows with age, he will become adept at recognizing your moods. As long as he always has his discipline and control kept sharp and you never fall into the temptation of giving him nothing to do from the end of one shooting season to the beginning of the next, he will easily cope with the dual role of working dog and pet. In fact, you will gain greater reward from your dog as you get to know him as a character and personality, and as the unique bond between you strengthens.

Excellent examples of this are easily seen. When my own children were small they used to cause great amusement by raising their arms in the air exactly as they had seen me doing, commanding dogs large enough to look them in the eye, to sit. To watch the dog, an expectant look on his face and his tail wagging, no one could doubt that he fully realized that this was a small child and they were playing a game together.

I was once on a camping holiday in a large multi-roomed tent, and my children thought it was great fun to have the two dogs lie flat on their backs between their beds. The dogs put up with a great deal of gentle abuse and would lie where the children expected them to, for all the world like large black teddy bears, albeit they kept one eye on me for approval. Yet these two dogs that would gambol with tennis balls, retrieve sticks from the sea and generally behave like perfect house pets, were in fact skilled, impeccably mannered gundogs.

Your dog asks little of you in return for lifelong hard work and friendship, and with a little consideration, kindness and good food, will give you all his loyalty and love – a relationship which is highly rewarding.

## The mature dog

What happens to well-trained gundogs as they mature? Are they like a good wine or a fine whisky and become better as they grow older, or are they more like fruit – ripening to perfection before starting to go off?

*An experienced Springer Spaniel picking up on the grouse moors.* (DAVID HUDSON)

Strange though it seems, a dog's behaviour and abilities vary with the breed. Spaniels, for example, tend to go back as they get older. Labradors, on the other hand, seem to maintain their training requiring only slight 'tweaking' by the handler.

## Spaniels

The mature Spaniel of five years and older can develop faults which in a young dog you would put down to the trainer moving too fast through its training, causing the training to unravel as the tasks are put together. It can be extremely frustrating, therefore, when these faults develop in the older – and previously near-perfect – dog.

Problems, such as a failure to pace himself (burning out after two hours), pulling on his quartering pattern, and selective deafness are unlikely to occur overnight. You will not take your dog on a Saturday shoot and find that he has suddenly regressed from the previous weekend. The dog will develop these annoying faults gradually, so gradually that you may not notice, or more likely will have ignored because you know the dog is steady and well-trained. In any case they are very minor and, in the overall scheme of things, not that important.

The owner of the mature Spaniel should be aware that he is likely to develop these minor bad habits. He may progressively take a little more ground and become a little less eager to listen as instantly as he would have done at three years old.

Another annoying fault that older Spaniels can develop – which in a trialling situation would be marked down, and on a formal shoot would be annoying and embarrassing – is giving the occasional squeak at a peg. At first you may put it down to over-enthusiasm and be tempted to be half-hearted in your reaction or, even worse, to ignore it. Do not. If you allow the dog to get away with making a noise while waiting for a retrieve you can find that over a period of a season the squeak will gradually lead to a full-blown ballad!

If you are aware of the possibility that your well-trained dog may acquire some annoying faults as it gets older, watch out for the signs and do something about it before the faults become habits. As I have stressed in earlier chapters you should always have the attitude that a little sharpening up will do neither you nor your dog any harm and don't be afraid to give him some training refreshers occasionally.

## Looking after the mature Spaniel

As they mature the physical well being of the working Spaniel should be looked after. Tiredness is one area to look out for. Some Spaniel trainers believe that the modern Springer Spaniel does not have the stamina it used to. This hereditary lack of stamina can be put down to top breeders training their dogs for trialling where they are expected to run at high speed for two twenty-minute bursts. This is exactly the opposite of what is expected on a day's shooting where a Spaniel should be prepared to pace himself over a full day. The older the dog the more likely these problems seem to occur.

To counter this lack of stamina you should not allow your mature dog to go hunting for a full day. It is far better to pull him into heel for ten minutes (let another Spaniel do the work) and then allow him to hunt for ten minutes. In this way you will force the dog to pace itself.

The more tired a Spaniel gets the slower he goes, the less responsive to commands and he will generally lose his pattern as it becomes bigger and bigger.

## Labradors

Unlike his shooting colleague the Spaniel, a five-year-old Labrador will tend to improve with age and should require less 'maintenance' work. As they gain in experience they intuitively know the difference between a working day and a training or play session. It can therefore be quite frustrating when you want to demonstrate (or more accurately show off) your impeccably trained Labrador and he proceeds to treat the demonstration with disdain, becoming slow, lethargic and generally unresponsive. He knows this is not serious and does not see why he should make the effort to retrieve a dummy when you both know he can do this with his eyes shut! The same dog, on seeing you dressed in your shooting clothes and knowing you are getting ready to go shooting will revert to the dog you know he is and behave the way you expect him to.

Mature, experienced Labradors can be a real bonus to their handlers. A good example of this was my Labrador dog, Bracken, whom I took wildfowling on many occasions. As we were sitting in our hide in the early morning waiting for the first flight of geese to come into our decoys I eventually stopped looking (or listening) for them myself. All I needed to do was keep an eye on Bracken. His reaction told me when he heard them coming, and from which direction. He would mark them when they fell – patiently waiting for the flight to be over – and would give me a scathing look if I missed! I rarely needed to speak to him, a slight nod of the head was all he needed when it was time to leave the hide and get on with his work.

Occasionally the Labrador's superior abilities can give rise to problems. For example, since he has more game-finding capability than the handler he may fail to stop on

*The older dog, like this yellow Labrador, will still work but may have to take things a little easier as the years pass.* (DAVID HUDSON)

the whistle. Being intelligent and canny, Labradors – even as mature dogs – will often 'try it on' with their handlers. This can manifest itself in many ways but in a shooting context one of the worst attributes a dog can develop is running in. If the dog gets away with it a few times he will begin to persist and the domino effect will occur. Within a very short period of time you can find that all your good training work has unravelled.

As with Spaniels, do not become complacent, and be aware of any minor problems which your dog may develop. Work on them early before they become major. Keep reinforcing discipline and understand that even the best dogs can benefit from a few basic training sessions – even if they think the lessons are beneath them! A few summertime dummy sessions will do no harm to you or your dog.

## Looking after the mature gundog

Older dogs, no matter what the breed, should be cared for differently to their younger counterparts. A working dog will not necessarily live a shorter life than a domestic dog. Indeed, it is possible that because the working dog is expected to remain active for longer, he will outlive his more inactive (and probably) more obese domestic brother.

*The white muzzle of this Irish Setter betrays her age as she cools off in a peaty burn after a busy day on the hill.* (DAVID HUDSON)

As the dog gets older it becomes more important to make sure that his physical needs are looked after. Regular worming and grooming are important – particularly for Spaniels whose coats can become matted and tangled with debris. After a day's shooting do not let your dog travel or go into his kennel still wet and dirty. Always take a towel to dry off excess moisture and when you return home if the dog lives outdoors, make sure his kennel is warm and dry.

A good way to keep up fitness levels in you and your dog is to take him cycling. This is not advisable on public roads, but if you have access to cycle paths or tracks that are off-road, it can be of great benefit to you both. The dog will soon pace himself to you and, if you have been monitoring his fitness, should have no problem keeping up. Remember however, if the dog seems to be flagging not to force him to keep to your pace. Slow down or even stop for five minutes to allow the dog to recover before continuing.

No matter what age the dog is you should make sure you feed him correctly. In the older dog this becomes more critical. Keep an eye on his weight. Older dogs should not be allowed to get fat, but nor should they be kept too thin. This is particularly important over the winter months when the dog will need energy for both working and keeping himself warm. If he is not getting enough food to do both adequately his long-term health will suffer.

As the dog gets older his food requirements will change. There are many excellent foods available for the older dog. I tend to shy away from the very expensive varieties, at the same time knowing that to go for the cheapest is actually a false economy. The all-in-one varieties are the best and those specifically designed for 'senior' dogs are very good. Dogs do not need to eat tins of dog food (an expensive way of feeding), but the occasional treat of cooked meat from the kitchen will do him no harm at all. If my dogs are going to be working hard in cold weather I will occasionally feed them cooked liver. They enjoy it and it is very good for them. When they are working I will step up their protein intake, cutting it back over the summer when they are 'resting'.

Depending on the type of shooting you do your dog should be able to work for you for many years. My Labrador, Shot, is now eleven and I would not take him for a full day's shooting, but he is still capable of doing a morning's work. Neither would I take him wildfowling – particularly if there was a lot of swimming to be done – but I do allow him the odd retrieve from water. He's not ready to retire completely just yet.

Because of the type of dogs they are and the sort of work they are expected to do, the working Spaniel deteriorates faster than the working Labrador. They are so full of enthusiasm for their work that they can easily burn themselves out and it is up to their owners to ensure that they are not asking too much of their dogs particularly as they grow older. I have a Springer Spaniel, Lynn, who is now a very mature lady of twelve. She is getting deaf and her eyesight isn't what it was, but she is still desperate to hunt and retrieve for anyone who will let her, to the point where I can only get her to go back into her kennel by throwing a stick or a ball in first!

Dogs are faithful and loyal companions who will give many years of good service if they are treated properly and looked after well.

# INDEX